Tough Questions
You're Afraid to Ask Your Pastor!

Seeking and Receiving Answers
For Life's Difficult Questions

*"Ask, and it will be given to you; seek, and you will find;
Knock, and it will be opened to you.
For everyone who asks receives, and he who seeks finds,
And to him who knocks it will be opened."*

Matthew 7:7-8

Daniel C. Rhodes

Destiny Navigators

Tough Questions You're Afraid to Ask Your Pastor
Copyright © 2013
Daniel C. Rhodes—Destiny Navigators, LLC
Printed in United States of America

All rights reserved. This book is protected by the copyright laws of the United States of America and may not be copied or reprinted for commercial gain or profit. All Scripture quotations are from the New American Standard Bible : 1995 update. LaHabra, CA: The Lockman Foundation. Any variation is noted in parenthesis.

ISBN-13: 978-1493625987
ISBN-10: 1493625985

Destiny Navigators, LLC
Decatur, GA

www.DestinyNavigators.org
DanCRhodes@DestinyNavigators.org

Dedication

To all the wonderful people of God I've had the privilege of pastoring across nearly four decades of pastoral ministry. To all those who have submitted questions through my website: your honest and heart-felt questions about the Bible, life and the world stirs my heart to search the Scriptures for God's answers in His Word. Unless we find answers in God's Word, our conclusions are only human opinions.

Acknowledgments

I am greatly indebted to the vast array of Biblical reference materials, commentators, Christian authors and Bible teachers that have formed a sound theological grid of Biblical truth and Christian thought in my life. Without that solid foundation, this book neither could have been written nor would it have properly represented the truth of Scripture.

Deep appreciation and gratitude is given to our youngest daughter, Anna Lindsey. Her skillful assistance in copy-editing this work for grammatical correctness and flow of thought is irreplaceable. I am especially honored for Anna to work on this project with me because she and her family live what I write, as does our oldest daughter, Jenny Querubin, and her family.

Tough Questions You're Afraid to Ask Your Pastor

Contents

Is It Okay To Ask God Tough Questions? 1

PART I: Questions and Perplexities About the Bible 5

1. What Does the Voice of God Sound Like? 7
   ❖ *How Will I Know if God Is Speaking to Me?*

2. Scientific Discoveries Verses the Bible 11
   ❖ *Do Cavemen Discoveries Disprove the Creation Account?*

3. Why is the Old Testament so Violent? 15
   ❖ *Would a Loving God Order His People to Go to War?*

4. Can Dead People Talk to Us? 19
   ❖ *What About Samuel Being Conjured Up in 1 Sam. 28:5-20?*

5. Slavery in the Bible 23
   ❖ *Why Didn't God Just Abolish It?*

6. Divorce and Remarriage in Scripture 27
   ❖ *Does God's Word Really Say Christians Can't Remarry?*

7. Faith Verses Medicine 31
   ❖ *Why Do We Need Doctors if We Have Faith in God?*

8. Angels, Demons, Vampires and Zombies! 35
   ❖ *What Should You Do if They Show Up?*

9. Can Christians Ever Lose Their Salvation? 39
   ❖ *What About Scriptures That Say You Can?*

10. Are There Some Sins that God Won't Forgive? 43
    ❖ *What About the "Unpardonable" Sin?*

Tough Questions You're Afraid to Ask Your Pastor

PART II: Questions and Dilemmas Regarding Life 47

1. Why Do Bad Things Happen To Good People? 49
   ❖ *Why Does God Allow Suffering in the World?*

2. What Happens To People Who Believe in God,
   But Not in Jesus? 53
   ❖ *Would a Good God Send Innocent People to Hell?*

3. Two Questions Concerning the Working of God's Power ... 57
   ❖ *Why Won't God Deliver Me From _____?*
   ❖ *What About Christians with Alzheimer's Disease?*

4. Same Sex Marriage and Gay Lifestyles 61
   ❖ *How Should a Christian Respond to These Issues?*

5. PTSD...Is It a Hopeless Struggle? 65
   ❖ *Or Is There Purpose Beyond the Pain?*

6. How Can I Find Meaning In Life? 69
   ❖ *Who Am I...Why Am I Here...Where Am I Going?*

7. What Happens to People When They Die? 73
   ❖ *Are They Just "Sleeping?" Do They "Hang Around?"
   Or Does Everyone Go Straight to Heaven?*

8. Are Generational Curses Real? 77
   ❖ *Should I Be Prayed Over to Break Curses in My Life?*

9. Paralyzed by Tough Decisions? 81
   ❖ *How Should Christians Make Good Life-Choices?*

10. Why Didn't God Answer My Prayers? 85
    ❖ *I Prayed to God But He Didn't Help Me.*

PART III: Questions and Problems
Concerning Church and Ministry 89

1. Do All Religions Lead to God? 91
   ✧ *Does God Care Which Faith I Choose to Follow?*

2. How Can I Share My Faith With Unbelievers? 95
   ✧ *How Can I Minister to Atheists or People Who Mock God?*

3. Can Women Serve as Leaders and Pastors in Church?............ 99
   ✧ *What About the Apostle Paul's Writings in 1 Tim. 2:9-15?*

4. If I'm Not Fulfilled at My Church, Is it Okay to Leave? 103
   ✧ *Do I Have to Wait for God to Release Me?*

5. Will God Continue to Bless Me Even if I Don't Tithe? 107
   ✧ *What If I Decide to Not Go to Church at all?*

6. Why Do Some Pastors Have Thousands of Followers
   While Others Only a Hundred or Less? 111
   ✧ *Are Smaller Churches Less Important Than Larger Ones?*

7. When Your Pastor Sins! 115
   ✧ *What Should Your Church Do?*

8. What Happens to Aging and Retired Pastors? 119
   ✧ *Are They "Pastor Emeritus" or "Pastor Superfluous?"*

9. Disqualified From Church Membership! 123
   ✧ *Should Pastors Ever Turn People Away from Church?*

10. Betrayals and Offenses Among Christians 127
    ✧ *How Should We Handle Them?*

EPILOGUE—*Discovering God's Answers for Yourself* 131

Tough Questions You're Afraid to Ask Your Pastor

Thoughts, Ideas or Other Questions to Ponder

Is It Okay...
To Ask God Tough Questions?

Absolutely Yes! But You Have to Be Ready for His Answer!

Listen intently; study diligently; and ask thoughtful questions. These are the ways that God intends for you to gain knowledge and wisdom. Our Lord is never offended by your honest questions...if you really desire to know truth. Listen to what He says in His word:

- *"If any of you lacks wisdom, let him ask of God, who gives to all generously and without reproach, and it will be given to him."*—**James 1:5**

- *"My son, if you will receive my words and treasure my commandments within you, make your ear attentive to wisdom, incline your heart to understanding; For if you cry for discernment, lift your voice for understanding; If you seek her as silver and search for her as for hidden treasures; Then you will discern the fear of the Lord and discover the knowledge of God. For the Lord gives wisdom; From His mouth come knowledge and understanding."*— **Proverbs 2:1-6**

However, you may not want to hear the answers that God gives. There's an amazing account in the first two chapters of Habakkuk. The prophet was bewildered and asked God a Tough Question. He wanted to know why all the wickedness and violence in his nation was allowed to continue unchecked. But Habakkuk wasn't prepared for God's answer. God told him He was about to raise up a pagan nation to overrun Judah, destroy their city and carry them away as captives! And He did! *So, do you really want to know answers to your Tough Questions? Prepare yourself for what you may not want to hear!*

Is It Okay to Ask God Tough Questions?

What Are Tough Questions?

Tough Questions arise when we come to an impasse in our thinking and reasoning and can't figure out an answer on our own. At times we hit "brick walls" in life or follow dead-end streets thinking they were clear paths to success and fulfillment. Tough Questions may be about our study of Scripture when we run across apparent conflicts with other passages or human experience. Other times, Tough Questions stem from tragic dilemmas in which there is no obvious solution or way out. They bring us to our knees with an impassioned plea for help from the Lord. We desperately need to understand what just happened, why it happened, what we should do and where we can go next. *We've run out of human answers and solutions, and will perish unless God steps into our lives, interprets our dilemma and shows us the way out.*

I have personally been there on more occasions than you can imagine. When Biblical dichotomies perplex my mind...I dig deeper into God's word. When life's twists and turns leave me reeling in dismay, I diligently search Scripture. When my ministry appears to be falling off a cliff, I turn to the word of God. Only there, in the Secret Place of God's written word, do I find the Living Word...Jesus, the Savior of my soul. **He does more than just answer my Tough Questions...He "restores my soul and guides me in the paths of righteousness."**

Why Are Some People Afraid to Ask Questions?

I've taught countless numbers of classes in Bible School with hundreds of students. In every group of people you'll find the aggressive and the passive, the extrovert and the shy, the inquisitive and the apathetic. Here are a few suggestions why some are less likely to ask questions than others. This may not fit your reason, but it will give you some things to think about.

Is It Okay To Ask God Tough Questions?

1. **You May Not Know the Right Questions to Ask.** When new knowledge is being introduced to a student, the course of study is unexplored territory and may be overwhelming. The student doesn't know enough to ask an intelligent question. When we run into a brick wall, we're probably stunned, confused and hurting. *We can't think straight and all we want to know is "What Just Hit Me?!"*

2. **You Don't Want to Appear Foolish.** Years ago after teaching a class, I asked there were any questions. It was as if I had been speaking a foreign language...they just looked at me with blank stares. Then I announced, *"The only stupid question is the one you don't ask...because you'll remain clueless if you don't!"* Hands began to timidly lift one by one. Many of us assume that everyone is smarter than we are. That's not true! *The question you ask may be the same one someone else wanted to ask but they were afraid of looking foolish!*

3. **You're Afraid of Being Embarrassed Publically!** When I was much younger, I was in a very unfortunate setting in which an arrogant teacher humiliated a fellow student for asking a basic question that had an obvious answer. Everyone laughed...except the one who asked the question. If this has ever happened to you, don't let it steal your desire to learn truth. **Like the Apostle James wrote,** *"God gives wisdom to all generously and WITHOUT REPROACH"* (James 1:5).

4. **You Don't Want to Put Your Pastor on the Spot...Or You Don't Want Your Pastor to Know Your Problems!** Many times I've received requests for appointments from parishioners of other churches. *When I asked why they didn't go to their pastor, their answer was one of two things: 1- My pastor is young and inexperienced; or 2- I don't want him to know the mess that I'm in.* Out of courtesy, I kept the appointment. But I encouraged them to speak with their own pastor as well.

5. **You May Not Want to Hear the Answer!** I've saved this one for last because it's probably the most soul-searching. It's the same reason some refuse to go to a doctor for a checkup. They're afraid of what the physician might discover! Jesus, in quoting Isaiah said, *"The heart of this people has become dull, With their ears they scarcely hear, And they have closed their eyes, Otherwise they would see with their eyes, Hear with their ears, And understand with their heart and return, And I would heal them"* (Matt. 13:14-15). **In other words, some don't want to hear God's answer because they would have to change the way they live.** Tragically, many who have counseled with me refused to follow Biblical answers and solutions to their questions and problems. They just didn't want to change!

But, Be Careful About Asking with Wrong Motives!

Jesus was the Incarnation of the Living God who came to earth to show people who God really is (John 14:5-11; Heb. 1:3). He was <u>THE ANSWER</u> to all who honestly wanted to know God and more about Him. But the Religious Leaders of Jesus' day had a different agenda. They wanted to defend their place of honor and authority in their Legalistic Religious System. They considered Jesus as threat and did everything to discredit Him (Luke 20:20-26). **There's a big difference between *Asking God Questions* and *Questioning Him!*** Here are a few examples of questions asked with wrong motives:

1. Questions trying to get approval for what you've already done.
2. Questions trying to justify your anger, bitterness or resentment.
3. Questions intending to prove heretical ideas about the Bible.
4. Questions trying to discredit the pastor or prove him wrong.

However, questions asked with an honest heart will most certainly receive forthright answers from the Lord. (Mark 12:28-34)

Part I: Questions and Perplexities About the Bible

Since we, as Christians, believe the Bible is God's word, it's essential that we read and understand what God is saying to us. Along the way, all of us run into questions concerning "apparent" contradictions in scripture or how passages relate to us and the world where we live.

Recently I invited those who follow my ministry to send me "Tough Questions" that they couldn't find answers to or that they've always wondered about. Some of these questions were suggested by fellow pastors who know what their parishioners struggle with. Unfortunately, these issues can, at times, be used to divide believers into doctrinal camps. *The intention of this book is not to divide, but to provide Biblical answers for your consideration.* Since this is not an exhaustive list, I selected ten essential questions and addressed them based on proven exegetical methods and my understanding of Scripture.

<u>Note</u>: One question that is not included in this book is, *"Where Did the Bible Come From and Why Do We Believe It Really Is God's Word?" Since the Bible declares that Scripture <u>IS</u> God's word (2 Pet. 1:19 NIV; 2 Tim. 3:15-17), this is the primary presupposition from which all answers to Tough Questions flow.*

Part I: BIBLE Questions

Thoughts, Ideas or Other Questions to Ponder

Part I: BIBLE Questions

Bible Question 1

What Does the Voice of God Sound Like?

How Will I Know If God Is Speaking To Me?

Tough Question

"I've read in the Bible that God spoke to people like Adam and Eve, Noah, Moses, Samuel and the Prophets. *Does God still speak to people like that today? And if He does, what does His voice sound like and how will I know if He is speaking to me?*"

Thinking Deeper

- ❖ If God Spoke to Me, What Would He Say?
- ❖ What Does God's Voice Really Sound Like?
- ❖ How Can I Know If It's Really God's Voice or Not?

Part I: BIBLE Questions

Answers Discovered in God's Word

When God Speaks, He Reveals Himself and His Redemptive Purpose For Your Life.

God exists in a totally different realm than our human time-space world. God is Spirit, infinite and eternal while we are finite and mortal. Tragically, because of sin, we are further separated from God. Thus it's impossible for human beings to know God, much less to relate to Him. That's why He appeared in the Old Testament as <u>wind</u>, <u>fire,</u> <u>clouds</u> and <u>storms</u>. He spoke to people and prophets through <u>visions</u> and <u>angels</u>. **God's Ultimate Purpose for appearing or speaking to people was RESTORATION**...how He redeems fallen humankind and restores them back to Himself! *The greatest Self-Revelation of God was when He became flesh, dwelt on the earth and <u>Redeemed</u> us. That's who the Lord Jesus Christ was and is! (Heb. 1:1-4)*

What Does God's Voice Really Sound Like?

1. **God Is Living and Personal.** He is not a personification of a human philosophy. He reveals Himself to each person in a way that relates specifically to them. And language is not a problem for God. *When He speaks, His words penetrate beyond our minds and hearts and enter into our human spirits (Heb. 4:12).*

2. **God's Voice Sounds Like Your <u>PASTOR'S</u> Voice When He or She Is Anointed for Preaching and Teaching.** God stirs pastors' hearts with specific messages for His people. Listen carefully so that you won't miss what God is saying to you (Rom.10:13-17).

3. **God's Voice Sounds Like a True <u>PROPHETIC</u> Word Spoken to You.** Prophets speak forth the heart and mind of God (2 Pet. 1:21). Don't discount true prophecy (1 Thess. 5:19-21). It's how the Lord edifies, exhorts and comforts you (1 Cor. 14:3).

Part I: BIBLE Questions

4. **God's Voice Sounds Like <u>YOUR</u> Voice When You Read His Word.** The Bible is the written self-revelation of God's kind intentions for you (2 Tim. 3:15-17). If you're not regularly reading God's word, you're shutting out His voice from speaking directly into your heart!

5. **At Times, God Speaks Through Life's <u>CIRCUMSTANCES</u>.** Not every good or bad experience is God speaking to you. But for the Spirit-led believer, this is one of the ways He warns, guides and teaches you what's best for you (Ps. 37:23-24; Is. 48:17 NIV). Carefully consider the experiences you have in life and ask the Lord if He's speaking to you through them.

How Can I Know If It's Really God's Voice or Not?

1. **First of All...God's Voice Will <u>NEVER</u> Be In Opposition to His Written Word (the Christian Bible).** God does not contradict Himself. Research Scripture diligently and check with your pastor before you act on what you think you're hearing.

2. **God's Voice Strengthens, Encourages and Comforts You (1 Cor. 14:3 NIV).** When God speaks to you, He <u>quiets your confused mind</u> and brings <u>peace to your anxious soul</u>. He <u>restores your life</u> back to His purpose (Ps. 23).

3. **God's Voice Stirs Your Heart and Motivates Your Spirit for His Cause.** When God speaks, He breathes life into you, electrifies your soul and empowers you to accomplish <u>His</u> purposes...not just things for your own personal gain (Ex. 35:21-22; Hag. 1:14).

4. **God's Voice Puts You Back on Track with Him and Your Destiny.** At times we all get off our course and slip away from the Lord's intentions. Like the last words that Jesus spoke to the seven pastors and churches, *He will <u>Commend</u> you, <u>Correct</u> you, <u>Counsel</u> you and <u>Challenge</u> you! (Rev. 2-3)*

Part I: BIBLE Questions

What Does This Answer Really Mean to You?

1. **God's Voice Is More Important Than Natural Food!** People can't live without food. And neither can true Christians live without the Voice of God speaking regularly into their lives. *God's word (either read or spoken) is spiritual food for those who hunger and thirst for righteousness (Matt. 4:4; 5:6).*

2. **You Must Listen Intently for God's Voice.** Have you ever read in scripture about having "Ears to Hear" what God is saying? This means many people are spiritually deaf and cannot hear the voice of God. Seek first the Kingdom of God and His righteousness and He will give you a "hearing heart." *Then you will be astounded at how often God will speak to you!*

3. **When God Speaks to You, He Shows You How Much He Loves You and Is Aware of You.** When you consider how breathtaking our God is and how far we've strayed from His purposes, it amazes us how personal He really is. *When you sense God's voice in your life, the only proper response it to worship Him and serve Him all the days of your life!*

Thoughts, Ideas or Other Questions to Ponder

_____

_____

_____

_____

_____

_____

Part I: BIBLE Questions

Bible Question 2

Scientific Discoveries Verses the Bible

*What About Cavemen and Neanderthals?
Do These Discoveries Disprove the Creation Account?*

Tough Question

"There is scientific evidence that a race of primitive people known as "cavemen" existed on earth. I've read they did not have a spoken language and therefore only communicated with pictures and grunts. However, the Bible tells us that Adam and Eve were the first people created, and they DID understand and speak a language to God (i.e. Adam gave names to all the animals and later they tried to explain to God why they ate the forbidden fruit). *Please explain how both of these scenarios can be true.*"

Thinking Deeper

- ✧ Who Interprets Scientific Discoveries and What Is Their Presumption?

- ✧ What Does God's Word Say About Prehistoric People?

- ✧ How Should a Christian Interpret Anthropological Discoveries According to God's Word?

Part I: BIBLE Questions

Answers Discovered in God's Word

As you know, the Bible is not a book of science, history or philosophy. It is the self-revelation of God. It tells us who He is, what He does, how people got into trouble and how God rescues those who trust in Him. *The people and events in Scripture are selectively recorded by the Holy Spirit for the purpose of showing us God's redeeming grace toward humankind...not for validating or refuting scientific theories.* Yet, God's word does give insight that will lead us to an answer to your question. **But a deeper question must first be asked and answered: "Who interprets scientific discoveries and what is their presupposition?"** A presupposition is a necessary assumption or background belief without which a conclusion cannot be made.

Now we can address who "Prehistoric" people were and how Christians should view scientific discoveries.

1. **The Bible Clearly Reveals the Intelligence of "Prehistoric" People.** Prehistoric simply means that people and events existed before history was recorded in written languages. Adam and Eve were the first "prehistoric" people on earth. As you mentioned in your question, they were created in God's image with intellectual abilities to rule the earth, name the animals and respond to God (Gen. 1-3).

2. **The Idea That Prehistoric People Were Lower Forms of Humans Who Couldn't Talk Is a <u>THEORY</u>, Not Fact!** Charles Darwin's "The Origin of Species" published in 1859 led the scientific world to believe that humans are simply another form of animal that might have evolved...quite possibly from apes. *Darwin's mother and wife were Unitarians who rejected the validity of the Bible and the concept of the Trinity.* In Darwin's later life, he became an agnostic and wrote, *"the Bible is no more to be trusted than the sacred books of the Hindus or the beliefs of any barbarian."*

Part I: BIBLE Questions

3. **Consequently, Modern Science Interprets Anthropological Discoveries Based on a Theory of a Man Who Rejected Both the Bible and God!** Instead of viewing cave drawings as early forms of art, they presume that they represent a lower form of humans who couldn't talk. Then, with that presupposition, they hire artists to depict prehistoric men and women as half human and half ape!

4. Gaining Further Insight From God's Word:
   - ✧ **Actually, the Bible tells of some people who did live in caves...but that didn't mean they were illiterate.** Job 30:3-7 describes outcasts of society. Even David once lived in a cave (1 Sam. 22:1).

   - ✧ **Rejecting God and His Word lead to all forms of distorted thinking.** Exchanging God's truth for a lie (Jer. 2:13) corrupts every aspect of human life (Rom. 1:20-32; Eph. 4:17-19).

   - ✧ **Accepting unbelievers' theories instead of Biblical accounts leads to further unbelief** (1 Tim. 6:20-21; 2 Tim. 2:15-18; 3:13-17). If you can remove God's creation account from Scripture, you can also remove His Salvation account! Believing God created men by evolution is just as foolish (Col. 1:15-16).

What Does This Answer Really Mean to You?

1. **It Means That You Are a Special Creation of God Made in His Image and Likeness.** You are not just an organism that evolved into a higher creature by a blind process of nature and then crawled out of some prehistoric pool. God created you, loves you and cares about everything that happens in your life.

Part I: BIBLE Questions

2. **You Can Be Confident That God Has a Special Purpose and Plan for Your Life...Even Before You Were Born.** He desires a personal relationship with you and is continually revealing Himself to you. He is guiding and directing your life toward a wonderful Destiny in Him (Jer. 1:5; Ps. 139:13-17).

3. **When Your Life Is Over, It Means That You're Not Like an Animal Whose Life Dies With Them.** Because God created you in His image, your soul and spirit will never die. Those who place their trust in the Savior will live forever in Heaven with Him.

Thoughts, Ideas or Other Questions to Ponder

Bible Question 3

Why Is the Old Testament So Violent?

Would a Loving God Command People to Go to War?

Tough Question

"Our family enjoys watching the History Channel's documentaries on the Bible. For us, it really brings to life the great Bible stories that I learned as a child. But I couldn't get over all the horrible violence that it portrayed. *Did God really approve of all that violence or did people misunderstand His Command and just take it too far?*"

Thinking Deeper

- ✧ Are There Some Aspects About God's Character That I Might Not Understand?

- ✧ What Does Righteous Justice Really Mean?

- ✧ Is the God of the Old Testament Different Than Who I See in the New Testament?

Part I: BIBLE Questions

Answers Discovered in God's Word

First of All, Unless You Understand God's Character, You'll Never Understand This Answer

1. **God Is Holy, Righteous and Just.** God is everything we are not. There is <u>NO</u> limit to His moral purity. He justly judges all that is evil and deals with iniquity according to His righteousness character.

2. **Yet, God Is Love...Merciful and Patient.** God's unconditional Love is never frustrated by His Rightful Judgment against evil. He patiently waits for people to come to repentance, not wishing for any to perish (2 Peter 3:9).

3. **But God Is Not Blind to Sin.** God's infinite Righteousness cannot simply overlook sin regardless of how "minor" we think it is. Even Jesus was clear about this in Matt. 5:17-48. There is nothing hidden from His eyes...*that's why we desperately need the Savior (Heb. 4:13-16)!*

Next, You Have to Realize What Happened to People

1. **Freedom of Will, Not God, Brought Violence and Death.** God warned Adam what would happen, but he failed to listen (Gen. 2:16-17). When <u>unrepentant</u> corruption and violence filled the earth, His heart was grieved. *God's Judgments are always Righteous, even if He destroys wicked people (Gen. 6:5-13).*

2. **People Who Love Evil and Hate Righteousness Receive Judgment <u>ACCORDING</u> to Their Deeds.** Violent people who are merciless will receive no mercy (Ezek. 7:27; James 2:13). If you live by the sword, you'll die by the sword. That's called Righteous Justice! *Even Jesus said this (Matt. 7:2; 26:52).*

3. **So, Don't Misdirect Your Compassion to the Incorrigible.** The nations of Canaan were some of the most sexually perverted, morally depraved, and bloodthirsty people of all ancient history...they even burned their children alive as sacrifices to pagan gods! *For this reason, God's judgment came upon them to remove their ungodly influence from the land (Ex. 23:23-24; Deut. 18:9-14; Ps. 106:34-41).*

However, "War" (Intense Physical Fighting) in the Old Testament Was Redirected in the New Testament

1. **Israel, in the Old Testament, Was a Nation-State Living in a Barbaric World of Warlords.** Force was the only thing enemies of God feared or respected. When they were defeated, they knew that Israel's God <u>was</u> and <u>is</u> GOD (Ex. 12:12-13; 14:4)!

2. **In God's NEW Covenant with Us (Heb. 8:8-13), He Defeated Our Greatest Enemy...SIN!** When the Lord sent His Son, He fought and won the greatest war ever to set us free from sin. *Now, our task is to live in that freedom (Rom. 8:1-14).*

3. **Both the Old and New Testaments Demonstrate God's LOVE <u>and</u> His JUDGMENT.** God's love has always been the motivation for deliverance (Deut. 7:7-8; John 3:16). His judgments are righteous...then, now and in the future (Eccles. 12:14; 1 Pet. 4:17; Rev. 20:11-15). *But what happened to CHILDREN of evil people in the Old Testament when they were killed or died?* Before the age of accountability, their place in heaven was eternally secure (Luke 18:16; 1 Cor. 14:20). That's God's merciful character.

Part I: BIBLE Questions

What Does This Answer Really Mean to You?

1. **You Don't Have to Worry About a World That Appears to Be Careening Out of Control.** God will most certainly judge all that is evil and reward those who walk in His righteousness.

2. **It Doesn't Mean That Our Nation Should Abolish Our Military.** There's nothing wrong with protecting our country against aggression with modern weaponry and armies. But our trust should be in God's justice that overthrows evil through us rather than our military might alone (Prov. 21:31).

3. **You Can Have Confidence That the Lord Has Already Won Your War Against Sin.** He will protect you from all evil and will ultimately rescue you and bring you to heaven (2 Tim. 4:18).

Thoughts, Ideas or Other Questions to Ponder

Part I: BIBLE Questions

Bible Question 4

Can Dead People Talk to Us?

What About When Samuel Was Conjured Up From the Grave and Spoke to King Saul?

Tough Question

"Recently I read a perplexing passage in 1 Sam. 28:5-20. Saul, the first king of Israel, went to a medium who could call up spirits from the dead. Saul asked the woman to call up the prophet Samuel from the grave. Though sorcery was forbidden by God, I was amazed that Samuel actually appeared and spoke to Saul! How could that be? ***Was it really Samuel or a demon playing tricks on Saul? What actually happened?***"

Thinking Deeper

- ✧ Is the Supernatural Realm Real...Or Is it Like a Fictional Sci-Fi Thriller?

- ✧ What Really Happened in the Story of Saul, the Medium and Samuel?

- ✧ What Does This Mean for You and Me...3,000 Years Later?

Part I: BIBLE Questions

Answers Discovered in God's Word

Many people are fascinated by the supernatural. That's why there are so many movies and TV shows about it. But this story isn't a Sci-Fi thriller. *It's a real account of a rebellious king, his foolish actions and tragic end.*

The Realm of the Supernatural Is More Real Than You Think!

1. **The Supernatural Lies Just Beyond Our Natural Senses.** It's the realm of God, angels and evil spirits (Col. 1:16-17). You can't see it, but it's all around you. *Not only that...you can enter into it!*

2. **There Are Only Two Supernatural Realms...Good and Evil.** Satan's kingdom of evil constantly tries to lure people into his world. *But God warns us that Satan's kingdom is doomed... forever (1 John 2:15-17).*

3. **There Are Two Doors to the Supernatural: One Leads to Life, the Other to Death.** Seeking to know your future apart from God and His wisdom, leads to death. That's what happened to Adam and Eve (Gen. 3:1-24).

So, What Happened With Saul, the Medium and Samuel?

1. **Saul's Actions Were "Dead" Wrong (Deut. 18:10-14)!** Dead people can't appear or talk to you (Luke 16:26)...but Satan and evil spirits can! (Gen. 3:4-5; 2 Cor. 11:13-15). *If you listen to people who inquire about your future from spirits, you'll end up just like they are...Spiritually DEAD!*

2. **Was the Apparition a Satanic Counterfeit or a Vision From God?** In this story, the medium was just as shocked as Saul when Samuel appeared. Whether it was an evil spirit sent by God (2 Chron. 18:20-22) or a divine vision, the matter was from the Lord. *One final time, God repeated His judgment upon Saul.*

3. **Caution! If God Isn't Speaking to You, Repentance Is Your Only Option!** Saul knew that God had departed from him. But instead of repenting, he sought an answer from a forbidden source. *Walking through the wrong door into the supernatural is catastrophically tragic (1 Sam. 31:2-6)!*

What Does This Mean for You and Me...3,000 Years Later?

1. **Slam Shut Every Door to the Supernatural That Is Not Through Jesus.** Even seemingly "innocent" things like horoscopes, signs of the zodiac and Ouija board games lead you away from God. *Be Careful! If you seek after the forbidden, God may give you what you want! (2 Thess. 2:8-12)*

2. **Neither Should You Be Overly Fascinated With Angels.** Angels are supernatural beings assigned to minister to believers (Ps. 91:11). They can appear to people...BUT they are far inferior to Jesus (Heb. 1:3-14). *God warns us to not give them glory instead of God (Col. 2:18-19; Rev. 22:8-9).*

3. **Jesus Is the Only Door to God (John 14:6), Your Future (Mark 10:28-30) and Heaven (John 14:1-3).** When you are born again by the Spirit of God, He gives you spiritual gifts that allow you to function in the Realm of God's Spirit for the edification of the church (1 Cor. 12; 13; 14). All other doors are satanic in origin. *However, with God's power and protection, you can withstand and war against evil forces that operate in the supernatural realm (Eph. 6:12-18; 2 Cor. 10:3-6).*

Part I: BIBLE Questions

Thoughts, Ideas or Other Questions to Ponder

Bible Question 5

Slavery in the Bible

Why Didn't God Just Abolish It?

Tough Question

"Here's an issue I've been struggling with for years. **Why wouldn't Paul write to Christian slave owners to set their slaves free since they had become part of the new creation in God's Kingdom?** Why do some passages that he wrote seem to perpetuate slavery among men, while in others passages, he declares 'there is neither bond nor free' in Christ?"

Thinking Deeper

- ✧ What Was It Like to Be a Slave During Bible Days?

- ✧ So, Why Didn't Jesus Just Abolish Slavery?

- ✧ What Happened? I Thought the Kingdom of God Made All Things New!

Part I: BIBLE Questions

Answers Discovered in God's Word

What Was It Like to Be a Slave During Bible Days?

1. **It Was NOT Like Slavery in America.** In America's shameful past, slavery was the ungodly practice of slave trading...the capturing, deporting and selling of human beings purely for profit with no regard to their humanity or personal welfare. Neither God nor Scripture ever approve of this kind of atrocity.

2. **Slavery in the Old Testament.** Though slavery in our modern world is repugnant, it was an accepted social institution in the ancient world. Slaves functioned more as domestic servants than as an economic industrial engine. Other than the involuntary slavery of war prisoners (Num. 31:25-27, 47), a Hebrew debtor or indigent could resort to voluntary self-sale (Lev. 25:39-41). In some cases, a slave may choose to remain with his master whom he loved (Exod. 21:5-6). *God's Law sought to regulate the existing custom of slavery, require humane treatment, and set terms of release rather than abolish it. (Ex. 21:2-4, 26-27).*

3. **Slavery in the New Testament.** Neither Jesus nor His disciples had any part in the system of slavery. The New Testament never once encouraged the dehumanizing practice of **slave trading**. Instead, it focused on the **relationships** between slaves and their masters (Eph. 6:5-9; Col. 4:1). *And Paul urged Philemon to treat his runaway slave as a brother in the Lord rather than as a slave (Philem. 15-16).*

So, Why Didn't Jesus Just Abolish Slavery?

1. **God Is Not a Micro-Manager of Our Conduct.** In God's wisdom, He leaves room for the process of moral maturity and self-reformation. Once we come to the full knowledge of being

rescued from the kingdom of darkness and transferred to the Kingdom of God's Son, our wrong behavior becomes self-evident! *God would rather gently lead you by His Spirit than with a bit and bridle (Ps. 32:8-9).*

2. **Jesus and Paul Used the Concept of Slavery as a Profound Teaching Tool of the Kingdom.** Jesus actually performed the work of a slave as an example for His disciples to follow (John 13:4-17). He used the parable of a king and a slave to illustrate mercy and forgiveness (Matt. 18:23-35). Paul called himself a slave (bondservant) to God and then contrasted it with slavery to sin (Rom. 1:1; 6:17-23).

The Kingdom of God Does Not Create an Instantaneous Utopian Society.

1. **Maturing Takes Time...Sometimes Generations!** As with learning to accept women in church leadership, it takes time. It took John Newton, the Slave Ship captain who wrote "Amazing Grace," **20 years after his conversion** to stop slave trading and work to abolish slavery in England.

2. **God's Kingdom Changes Our Hearts...Regardless of Our Social Standing.** Life is not fair! Some are born into affluence and others into poverty. God may not deliver you from the ruling class in society, but He will give you full access to Himself and His Grace (Col. 3:22-25; 1 Tim. 6:1-2; 1 Pet. 2:18-24).

3. **In Christ, There Are No Social Disparities (Gal. 3:27-29).** A slave doesn't have to be physically emancipated to be free in Christ (1 Cor. 7:20-24). However, when redeemed attitudes rule in hearts, it becomes obvious that the Christian Gospel and Human Slavery are irreconcilable.

Part I: BIBLE Questions

What Does This Answer Really Mean to You?

1. **It Means You Must Thoroughly Research Bible Passages that "Appear" to Conflict with Your Sense of Morality.** Before jumping to conclusions and questioning the Bible, it's crucial to set passages in the proper context in which they were written. *(See the Epilogue at the end of the book to learn how to study God's word and find answers for yourself.)*

2. **You Can Learn From the Biblical Concept of Slavery.** We who have been freed from slavery to sin, never have to return to it again (2 Pet. 2:20-22). *But to be a "slave" to God and righteousness, results in sanctification and eternal life (Rom. 6:17-22)!* That kind of "slavery" is good!

3. **You Can Be a Catalyst for Change.** As you learned, God doesn't change society overnight. He leaves many aspects of our broken world for us to reform. Look around and ask the Lord how you can be His agent for change. If you see evil influences at work in your neighborhood, town, city or government, do something about it. *Remember, God changes things by shining His light though you...even from <u>WITHIN</u> the dark kingdoms of the world (2 Cor. 4:6).*

Thoughts, Ideas or Other Questions to Ponder

_____

_____

_____

_____

_____

Part I: BIBLE Questions

Bible Question 6

Divorce and Remarriage

Does God's Word Really Say Christians Can't Remarry?

Tough Question

"Are there any biblical guidelines for Christians to follow who have experienced the devastation of divorce and desire to begin a new relationship that may lead to remarriage? *I've been told that divorce is a sin and that to marry again is adulterous. Is divorce really unforgivable? Will it disqualify me from church leadership?*"

Thinking Deeper

- ✧ What Was the Bible Talking About When Malachi Wrote that "God Hates Divorce?"

- ✧ What's the Real Story Behind Why Jesus Said that Marrying After Divorce Is Adultery?

- ✧ What Should Divorced Christians Do if They Want to Remarry?

Part I: BIBLE Questions

Answers Discovered in God's Word

1. **Marriage and Divorce Have Deeper Meanings Than Most People Realize.** Marriage is a sacred covenant symbolic of the spiritual relationship between God and His people (Eph. 5:22-32). When marriage vows are broken through unfaithfulness or hardness of heart, it leads to divorce (Matt. 19:7-9). So it is when a person's heart becomes hardened against God. *Forsaking God's love and running after evil is seen by God as Spiritual Adultery (Ezek. 6:9). Spiritual Divorce is walking away from your Covenant with God.*

2. **God Hates the <u>UNFAITHFULNESS</u> That Causes Divorce (Mal. 2:16).** In this passage, God was addressing men who were divorcing believing wives and marrying pagan women. This caused unfaithfulness to God by mixing world religions with their faith in the one true God. *Since God is unswervingly faithful to His covenant, He requires marriages to have the same high level of commitment to one another.*

3. **Why Did Jesus Say that Marrying After Divorce Is Adultery in Matt. 5:32?** In the 5th chapter of Matthew, Jesus was addressing a broken religious system that believed righteousness was attainable by keeping the Law (Matt. 5:20). For those who thought they were guiltless because they hadn't committed <u>physical</u> adultery, Jesus revealed that adultery actually begins in the <u>heart</u> of a person (Matt. 5:27-28). In response to the religious legalists who wanted to divorce and remarry for <u>ANY</u> cause, Jesus said that was adultery too (Matt. 19:3-9)! *That's why we need the Savior! Knowing that it's impossible for us to live a sinless life, Jesus perfectly obeyed the Law <u>for</u> us and gave us <u>His</u> righteousness (2 Cor. 5:21)...even if you marry after divorce.*

Part I: BIBLE Questions

4. **So, Can God Forgive Divorce and Give You a New Life?** Absolutely Yes! The only unforgivable sin is totally rejecting the work of the Holy Spirit and attributing it to evil. That's because the Holy Spirit is the One who applies the saving grace of Christ's atonement to our lives (Matt. 12:31-32). *__ALL__ other sins can be forgiven when you seek forgiveness, repent and receive Christ's redeeming grace (1 John 1:9).*

5. **Does Divorce Disqualify a Christian from Leadership in Ministry?** Some point to 1 Tim. 3:2, 12 and Titus 1:6 and say, "Yes!" Others believe these passages just describe a faithful family man who isn't a polygamist. However, Eph. 4:7-13 gives no restrictions for called leaders. *If God restored His people <u>after He divorced them</u> (Jer. 3:8; Hosea 2:7, 14-17), He can certainly restore a divorced and remarried person to ministry...even a pastor to the pulpit again!*

The Practical Side of Restoration

1. **Seek Competent Counsel.** Restoration is a process of learning how to live again. Since divorce is seldom the failure of one person, learn <u>why</u> your marriage failed and <u>how</u> to prevent future failures. *Don't make the same mistakes twice!*

2. **Your Children Are Your Top Priority!** It's impossible for children of divorce to escape without scars. Divorcing parents are still their children's parents. *Lay down your hostilities and love your children. If you don't, you'll lose them!*

3. **Finally, Your New Beginning Is in Your Hands.** If you are willing to receive God's redeeming love and cleansing grace (Ps. 103:10-14; 1 John 1:7-9), then there is no reason why you can't enter into a godly relationship that may lead to a covenant of marriage. *But if you want to hold on to a legalistic interpretation of divorce, you will live a very lonely life riddled with guilt and regret.*

Part I: BIBLE Questions

What Does This Answer Really Mean to You?

1. **It Means God Won't Punish You for Making a Mistake in Marriage.** Some marriage commitments are made before people are emotionally mature enough to sustain their unions. Others are forced because of pregnancies or social pressures. A failed marriage is tragic...but it's no worse than other sins for which Christ died. ***Seek forgiveness and move forward in Him.***

2. **But, You Can't Jump In and Out of Marriages At Will.** Repeated marriage failures are signs of deep emotional and spiritual immaturity. Unless major life-changes are made through counseling and spiritual restoration, you will leave a path of destruction for everyone involved...***especially children!***

3. **However, We Must Closely Examine Our Covenant with God.** Behavior really <u>does</u> matter...not in a legalistic way, but as an indicator that we belong to Christ. Remember, true faith is revealed by our conduct (2 Cor. 13:4-5). If we think we can willfully sin because Christ died for our sins, then our faith isn't faith at all...***it's presumption and self-justification! (Rom. 6:1-7)***

Thoughts, Ideas or Other Questions to Ponder

Part I: BIBLE Questions

Bible Question 7

Faith Verses Medicine

Why Do We Need Doctors If We Have Faith In God's Power To Heal?

Tough Question

"I read a news story about a Christian couple who thought that praying for their sick child rather than seeking medical help was a greater sign of faith. Tragically, their young child died. Does the Bible say that faith is better than medicine? ***Why are some people healed through prayer and others are not?***"

Thinking Deeper

- ✧ Does God Really Heal People...Even Today?

- ✧ Is There a Conflict Between Faith and Medicine?

- ✧ Are There Things We Must Do In Order to Receive God's Supernatural Healing?

Tough Questions You're Afraid to Ask Your Pastor   31

Part I: BIBLE Questions

Answers Discovered in God's Word

First of All, God Can Do <u>ANYTHING</u>!

1. **There Is Nothing Too Difficult For God (Jer. 32:17).** If God created the heavens and earth with just a spoken word, He can easily send forth His word and heal His people (Ps. 107:20). If Jesus raised the dead (John 11:43-44), then healing the sick is a small thing...*with or without medicine!*

2. **The Bible Is Filled With Accounts of Supernatural Healing.** God healed through Old Testament <u>Prophets</u> (1 Kings 17:17-24; 2 Kings 4:32-37) and New Testament <u>Apostles</u> (Acts 3:2-8; 5:14-16; 19:12; 20:9-12). And Healing is a gift of the Holy Spirit given to the <u>Church</u> (1 Cor. 12:1-11; Mark 16:16-18).

3. **Healing Is a <u>SIGN</u> of God's Restoration...Even Today.** Before there was sin in the world, there was no disease or death. Tragically, the fall of humankind into sin brought sickness, disease and death upon the whole earth. By God's grace and compassion, He restores people to wholeness through the prayers of His Church (James 5:14-16). Remember, there are many kinds of sicknesses: physical, emotional and spiritual. *But the greatest healing of all is the restoration of our relationship with God.*

There Is <u>No</u> Conflict Between Divine Healing and Medicine

1. **It's a Mistake to Try to Pit Faith Against Medicine.** God can heal in many ways: <u>instantly</u> (Matt. 20:30-34); <u>progressively</u> (Mark 8:22-25); and by <u>blessing therapeutic procedures</u> (2 Kings 20:7; 1 Tim. 5:23). *Anything good that helps people, including medicine, is ultimately from God (James 1:17; 1 Tim. 4:4-5).*

2. **Faith Is Trusting God to Fulfill His Promises, Regardless of His Methods.** Our role is to believe God...not to dictate how we want Him to fulfill His promises. *Don't be like the arrogant Naaman who demanded HOW he should be healed (2 Kings 5:9-14)!* Trust God, go to the doctor and be a good patient.

Why Are Some People Healed Through Prayer and Others Are Not?

1. **The Faith of the <u>Person in Need of Healing</u> Is a Key Factor.** Faith believes that God is able and willing to heal. This is the kind of faith that God responds to (Matt. 9:27-30; Mark 10:46-52). *But the lack of faith can limit your ability to receive God's healing (Matt. 13:54-58; Luke 4:22-30).*

2. **At Times, the Faith of <u>Others</u> Is the Catalyst for Healing.** In some instances, there appeared to be no indication that the person who was healed had any faith at all. But his friends did (Matt. 8:5-10; 15:22-28; Mark 2:3-12)! *God honors the faith and compassion of those who have more faith than you.*

3. **But God's <u>Higher Purpose</u> Is the Deciding Factor.** God's ways are far beyond human understanding (Is. 55:8-9). He can choose to raise people up to continue their work in His Kingdom (Matt. 8:14-15; Acts 9:36-42). At other times, He might grant His Grace, instead of healing, as power to endure suffering for a higher cause (2 Cor. 12:7-10). *Or God may choose to work through medical doctors!* Ultimately, God heals in heaven when our course on earth is finished (2 Tim. 4:6-8; Rev. 21:4-5).

What Then Shall We Do?

<u>Believe</u> God's promises; *<u>Pray earnestly</u>* for healing; *<u>Speak life</u>* over death; *<u>Declare</u>* God's purpose and destiny; and *<u>Trust God</u>* for the results. *Don't put people on guilt trips for lack of faith. Trust God!*

Part I: BIBLE Questions

What Does This Answer Really Mean to You?

1. **It Means the Medical Industry Is an Agent of God to Improve Your Quality of Life.** Regardless of the faith (or lack of faith) of doctors, nurses or hospital staff, God gave them their abilities to diagnose and treat illnesses. *To reject their medical skills is to reject God's blessings for you and your family.*

2. **It Does <u>Not</u> Mean that You Can Leave God Out of Your Life and Trust Medicine Alone.** When an illness (even a minor issue) befalls you, pray and trust God to add His blessings to the physicians and medication they prescribe. *God gets involved in your life when you TRUST Him (Prov. 3:5-6).*

3. **You Should Diligently Pray for Others Who Are Stricken with Sicknesses or Diseases.** Who knows...perhaps the Lord will honor your faith and bring about healing for another. But if the person you're praying for doesn't recover, it's <u>NOT</u> your fault or your lack of faith! Neither should you get angry with God. *Just pray and trust God. He is infinitely more concerned and compassionate for others than you are!*

Thoughts, Ideas or Other Questions to Ponder

_____
_____
_____
_____
_____

Bible Question 8

Angels, Demons, Vampires and Zombies

What Should You Do If They Show Up?

Tough Question

"I've been a member of many kinds of churches. Some are typical Christian denominations that preach the Gospel and help people live from day to day. Others are into Deliverance...casting out demons and evil spirits. And now I hear that there are some who are claiming that **talking to angels** should be normal! **What's next...Vampires and Zombies?** What does God's Word say about these things?"

Thinking Deeper

- ✧ Vampires and Zombies? That's Ridiculous!

- ✧ But What About Demons...Are They Real?

- ✧ How About Angels...Should We Try to Talk to Them?

Part I: BIBLE Questions

Answers Discovered in God's Word

First, Let's Address the Bizarre: Vampires and Zombies!

It's not the movie version of these horror creatures that bothers me...it's the real-life **"blood suckers"** and **"brain eaters"** that do! Some people <u>drain</u> every bit of your life-energy with their problems. Others go after your mind to consume it with their false doctrines and philosophies. *And what's worse, if they infect you, you'll become one of them!* If these kinds of "Vampires" or "Zombies" show up, deal with them quickly and deliberately. *Just refuse to buy into their "Drama!" That's better than a stake in the heart or a chainsaw to the head!*

Are Demons Real?

1. **Demons Are Very Real!** Most Bible Scholars agree that demons are evil spirits...fallen angels who followed and served Satan when he rebelled against God in heaven. They and their leader were cast out of heaven to the earth (Rev. 12:4, 7-9). As the Hebrew word for demon indicates, they "ruin and destroy" human lives. *Their mission is to oppose God and to tempt and delude people into sin.*

2. **Can Demons "Possess" a Born Again Christian?** Demons are still at work in the world today causing violence, torment, physical limitations and self-destruction. But, there is no record in the Bible of evil spirits possessing a Christian. Unfortunately, the fallen nature of Christians can be influenced by evil. *If we don't guard our hearts, we can participate in the work of demons (1 Cor. 10:20-21; Eph. 5:6-11).*

Part I: BIBLE Questions

3. **What Should You Do If They Show Up?** Remember, Jesus defeated Satan and his angels for you; and He gave <u>YOU</u> authority over their power (Matt. 10:1). *If they show up in your life, here's what to do: 1-Submit to God; 2-Resist the devil and he will flee; 3-Cleanse yourself from their defilement (James 4:7-8).* Satan, his angels and all who follow them will eventually be utterly destroyed (Matt. 25:41)!

Should We Try to Talk to Angels?

1. **Who Are Angels and What Do They Do?** Angels are God's Heavenly Host...created spirit-beings who serve and worship God forever (Ps. 148:2, 5; Rev. 4:8-9). Some angels are agents of God's providential work sent to communicate His will to people (Luke 1:19; Heb. 2:2), minister strength and protection (Ps. 91:11-12; Heb. 1:13-14), and execute divine judgment upon evil (2 Sam. 24:16; Acts 12:23).

2. **Should We Seek After Angels?** Angels do have the ability to converse with humans (Judg. 6:12; Luke 1:19; Acts 27:22-25) and are sent by God to assist us in time of need (Dan. 3:28; Matt. 4:11). *BUT...God warns us to never worship them or seek divine favor from them (Col. 2:18; Rev. 19:4, 10).* However, we can appeal to **God** *(not to angels)* for angelic assistance (2 Kings 6:15-18; Matt. 26:53).

3. **What Should You Do If They Show Up?** As wondrous as they are, they are <u>NOT</u> a substitute for Jesus (Heb. 1:1-6). Nor do they take the place of the Holy Spirit, who lives in believers and directs our lives (John 14:16-27). They are merely instruments of God's power sent for His purpose and glory. *Listen to what they say...but always <u>test</u> their words with God's word (1 John 4:1-3; 2 Tim. 3:15-17). If you don't, you may be talking to demonic forces!*

Part I: BIBLE Questions

What Does This Answer Really Mean to You?

1. **As Unkind as This May Sound, You Have to Recognize "Vampire" and "Zombie" Tendencies in Your Friends and Family Members.** This tongue-in-cheek illustration may make you chuckle, but it's more true than you may want to realize. *This doesn't mean you should cut these people out of your life. But you must be aware of and limit their influence on you.*

2. **It Means That the Realm of the Supernatural Is More Real Than You Think!** You can enter into that realm through many doors. Demonic forces beckon you into their world with enticements of the flesh. But there's only <u>ONE</u> true "door" that leads to God. It's Jesus...the Shepherd of your soul (John 10:9-11)! *Refuse all other doors. They only lead to destruction!*

3. **You Have to Guard Your Heart (Prov. 4:23-27).** Always be aware that music you listen to, movies you watch, books you read, and video games you play, will open your soul to either good or evil. *Whatever influences you, can rule you!*

Thoughts, Ideas or Other Questions to Ponder

_____

_____

_____

_____

_____

_____

Part I: BIBLE Questions

Bible Question 9

Can Christians Ever Lose Their Salvation?

What About Scriptures That Say You Can?

Tough Question

"I love God and try to practice His word in my life. However, I've recently read some passages that have greatly disturbed me. In Hebrews 6:4-8 it speaks of Christians who have fallen away and cannot be brought back to repentance. ***Also, Hebrews 3:12-14 and 10:26-31 makes me fearful that I might do something foolish and lose out with God...including my salvation! Is this really true?*** Please help me better understand these passages."

Thinking Deeper

- Is It Possible to Think I'm Saved...But Actually I'm Not?

- What Do Salvation and Eternal Security Really Mean?

- So, What About Passages in the Bible that Say I Can Fall Away from God?

Part I: BIBLE Questions

Answers Discovered in God's Word

Some People Who <u>Think</u> They Are Eternally <u>SECURE</u>... May Be in for an Eternal <u>SHOCK</u>!

1. It's one thing to grow up in a Christian home, attend church, read the Bible on occasion, and say you are a Christian. *It's a totally different matter to have a personal encounter with the Living God and receive His Son as Savior of your soul (John 1:12).* It's like the difference between swimming in water saying you are a fish and actually being a fish! (Luke 13:23-28).

2. Jesus said, *"Not everyone who says to Me, 'Lord, Lord,' will enter the kingdom of heaven,* but he who does the will of My Father who is in heaven will enter. Many will say to Me on that day, 'Lord, Lord, did we not prophesy in Your name, and in Your name cast out demons, and in Your name perform many miracles?' And then I will declare to them, '<u>I never knew you;</u> depart from Me, you who practice lawlessness.'" (Matt. 7:21-23). *Eternal Security is this: Knowing the Savior and being known by Him!*

3. God's desire is for everyone to believe in His Son and inherit eternal life (John 6:39-40; 1 John 3:23). *But salvation is a Personal Heart-Relationship with the Lord Jesus, not just a mental or nominal consent (Is. 29:13).*

However, Those Who Really Do Belong to Christ Are Eternally Secure in Him.

1. **Salvation Is Based on Your <u>FAITH</u> in God's Son...Not on the Works You Do or Don't Do.** If you think that doing something foolish will exclude you from salvation, you've forgotten how you received Christ. *If you cannot be saved by works, how then can works disqualify you?* (Eph. 2:8-9; Rom. 3:28).

Tough Questions You're Afraid to Ask Your Pastor

Part I: BIBLE Questions

2. **God Doesn't Throw His Children Away When They Sin...He Corrects Them.** Every loving parent disciplines their children to teach them right from wrong. Likewise, God's loving discipline, though not pleasant, puts us back on track with Him (Heb. 12:5-11). *Once you experience God's love, you'll never fear eternal judgment...because it has been removed (1 John 4:17-18)!*

3. **"No One Can Snatch You Out of My Hand" (John 10:27-30).** These words of Jesus steady the most troubled heart and bring peace to the most insecure soul. *When you place and keep your faith in the hands of your loving Savior, you are eternally secure in Him...and in the Father!* (John 3:16)

So, What About Hebrews 3:12-14; 6:4-8 and 10:26-31? Doesn't This Say You Can Fall Away from God?

1. The book of Hebrews was written to Jewish Christians whose **faith was beginning to waiver** with a temptation to revert back to the Jewish religion. *Apostasy is not a sudden denial of God or a sinful act; it's a gradual departure from the faith.* If not corrected, the faith that holds a believer to Christ can die!

2. **Yes, You Are Eternally Secure When You Are IN Christ...But Beware of False Security (John 15:1-11).** If you think you can live any way you want just because you once prayed a sinner's prayer, be careful! *True Faith is <u>Alive</u> and filled with the work God calls you to do.* (Rom. 6:1-2; James 2:14-20)

3. **The Holy Spirit Is Your Best Friend!** He is your Helper who walks with you and lives in you (John 14:16-17; 16:7-15). If you are truly born again, your redemption is sealed by God's Spirit and He will never stop drawing you back to Christ when you get off track (Eph. 1:13-14). *Listen to Him, seek forgiveness, repent, and trust in Jesus. This is your assurance of eternal security!* (1 John 1:5-10)

Part I: BIBLE Questions

What Does This Answer Really Mean to You?

1. **You Can Live in Total Confidence and Peace with God.** If you are truly born again, you don't have to live in fear that God will disqualify you from heaven because you sinned. *Remember, your confidence is in what Jesus did for you, not in your human ability to TRY to live a sinless life! (1 John 3:20)*

2. **When You Really "Mess Up Big Time," Run To (Not Away From) God and He Will Receive You With Open Arms.** Jesus knows what it's like to be tempted by sin (Heb. 2:17-18). And even more than that, *He knows how to RESCUE you from the temptations that threaten your soul (2 Pet. 2:7-9)!*

3. **It Means You Can Help Other Christians in Their Walk With the Lord.** Because you know what it's like to be rescued from sin, you can encourage others with your story (2 Cor. 1:3-4). People who are trying to "hide" from God (like Adam and Eve), need to know that the grace of God in Jesus really works. *You, my friend, are a living example of that grace (1 Tim. 1:15-16).*

Thoughts, Ideas or Other Questions to Ponder

Bible Question 10

Are There Some Sins That God Won't Forgive?

What About the "Unpardonable" Sin?

Tough Question

"I'm sure you've been asked this a hundred times, but this is really bothering me. It's about the Unpardonable Sin. I've read in the Bible that if people 'Blaspheme' against the Holy Spirit, they can never be forgiven. *I've done terrible things in my life and so have my friends and family members. At times I'm afraid that our past sins have 'crossed the line' and we can never be forgiven! What can we do to not lose out with God?*"

Thinking Deeper

- ✧ What Is Sin and Redemption All About?

- ✧ Is There Really an "Unpardonable" Sin?

- ✧ What About Other People Who I Think May Have "Crossed the Line"?

Part I: BIBLE Questions

Answers Discovered in God's Word

About Sin and Redemption

You've asked a very honest question that deserves a forthright Biblical answer. And you're not the only one who has ever anguished over this issue. I'll begin by explaining a little about Sin and Redemption.

1. **Here's the <u>Bad</u> News...<u>ALL</u> Sin Leads to Death.** When Adam and Eve failed, sin became part of our nature (Gen. 2:17; 3:16-24). Sin is more than wrong actions...it's a destructive condition that separates us from God and leads to Physical Death, Spiritual Death and Eternal Death in Hell (Luke 16:19-31).

2. **The <u>Good News</u> Is That God Offers a Permanent Solution for Our Sin Problem!** Because of God's eternal love for fallen humankind, He personally paid the price for <u>ALL</u> our sins...past, present and future (1 John 1:9-2:2). In Christ, the eternal punishment for sin is removed (2 Cor. 5:17-21; 1 John 4:13-19).

3. **However, Forgiveness and Eternal Life Are <u>Very</u> Conditional!** ALL of your sins, regardless of how heinous or numerous they may be, are forgiven...IF YOU BELIEVE in what Jesus did for you (John 3:16-21, 36)! If you don't believe, confess your sins and receive forgiveness, there is no hope! (Mark 16:16)

So, Is There an "Unpardonable" Sin?

1. **Yes, But VERY FEW Have Committed It.** This sin makes conversion and pardon impossible. It consists of a <u>***conscious***</u>, <u>***willful***</u> and <u>***malicious rejection***</u> and <u>***slandering***</u> of the convicting work of the <u>**Holy Spirit**</u> in regard to His work of grace in Christ and <u>***attributing***</u> it out of hatred and enmity to the devil himself (Matt. 12:24-32). ***Rejecting the Holy Spirit is rejecting Redemptive Truth (John 16:13-15).***

Part I: BIBLE Questions

2. **Even "Unbelief" Is Not the Unpardonable Sin...<u>UNLESS</u> That Person Dies in Unbelief!** Amazingly, the great Apostle Paul said he had formerly been a *"blasphemer"* who *"acted ignorantly in unbelief."* If Paul, who called himself the "chief of sinners," received mercy, so can you (1 Tim. 1:13-16).

3. **Anyone Who Is Afraid They May Have Committed the Unpardonable Sin...<u>HASN'T</u>!** Had you committed that sin, you would have never asked or been concerned about it. But remember, God's redemptive grace doesn't give anyone a "license" to sin (Rom. 6:11-23). Live righteously because you <u>ARE</u> forgiven, not because you're trying to earn salvation.

What About Your Friends and Family Members?

1. **First of All, Strengthen Your Faith so You Can Be a Witness for the Lord.** Your witness to others is all about your confidence (faith) in what God has done for you. Find a church where you can be surrounded by believers and can learn God's word. This is how your faith grows (Eph. 6:10-18; 1 Tim. 6:11-12).

2. **God Wants You to Diligently Pray for Others.** Prayer is an earnest request to God for a deep concern. Pray for the lost...that they would come to the saving knowledge of Christ (John 5:24; Acts 3:19). Pray that you would be empowered by the Holy Spirit to be Christ's witness (Acts 1:8). *Pray that God will use your testimony to snatch people out of the fires of eternal destruction (Jude 22-23).*

What Does This Answer Really Mean to You?

1. **Sin Is a Very Destructive Force in Your Life.** It can eat away at your Christian witness and your confidence in the Lord. It can destroy your career and family. It can even cut short your life if you engage in harmful and addictive activities that cause disease and careless accidents. *Why should you open yourself to sin after the Lord has rescued you from it (2 Peter 2:19-22)?*

2. **But as a Christian, You Don't Have to Live in Fear of Losing Your Salvation.** Read again the answer to Bible Question # 8 on pages 35-38. *If you are truly a born again Christian, you can be assured that you will never commit the "Unforgivable" Sin.*

3. **It Means God Can Use Your Faith and Confidence in His Redeeming Love to Help Others.** As I mentioned at the beginning of this teaching, many struggle with this issue. Because you know how deep God's love is for people and how far He went to rescue us, you are qualified to bring peace to their hearts. *However, this isn't true for unbelievers! First of all, lead them to Christ, then into confidence in His saving grace.*

Thoughts, Ideas or Other Questions to Ponder

Part II: Questions and Dilemmas Regarding Life

Life is an amazing journey. Along the way we encounter joys, discoveries, great expectations, and pleasant experiences. There are exhilarating moments of accomplishment and satisfactions when challenges are met and overcome. But when life's unexpected twists, turns and tragedies catch us off guard, we can feel like we're careening out of control with no hope for recovery. When the unthinkable happens, we're left stunned and paralyzed by events that are totally beyond our ability to manage. That's when the Tough Questions begin to flood our minds. *What's going on? Why is this happening? What does it mean? What should I do?*

Some of life's questions are about other people's problems and the dilemmas they struggle with. *But when these issues hit home and arrive on your own doorstep, it's a whole different story!* You're no longer a spectator watching from the grandstands...you're right in the middle of the chaos trying to survive! You don't need nice opinions or good ideas...*you desperately need God to step into your world to help you interpret what's going on, give you hope, and show you solutions.*

God's written word (the Christian Bible) is where you discover answers to ALL of life's Tough Questions. As mentioned before, I recently invited those who follow my ministry to send me "Tough Questions" that they couldn't find answers to or that they've always wondered about. Some of these questions were suggested by fellow pastors who know what their parishioners struggle with. In each case, the responses I give in these teachings come from specific accounts or general principles found in God's word. *May the Lord open your heart to see the character of God, hear His eternal voice, and receive His Truth. Without God working in our lives, all of us are helpless and hopeless.*

Thoughts, Ideas or Other Questions to Ponder

Life Question 1

Why Do Bad Things Happen To Good People?

Why Does God Allow Suffering in the World?

Tough Question

"I've heard about Christians who suffer unjustly, die prematurely and experience great misfortune. I have friends and family members who are facing total devastation (even death) through no fault of their own. *I know that God is aware of them, but why does He let these kinds of things happen?"*

Thinking Deeper

- ❖ Since Suffering Is a Universal Problem, How Do Other Religions (or Even Atheists) Deal With It?

- ❖ Does the Bible Explain Why Bad Things Happen In Life?

- ❖ How Should Christians Interpret Suffering When It Befalls Them?

Part II: LIFE Questions

Answers Discovered in God's Word

The presence of suffering poses problems in all generations from all walks of life. This includes Christians, people from the religions of the world and those who don't believe in God or aren't sure if there is a God. Some try to deal with suffering through a human philosophy of enlightenment and selflessness. Others think they are paying the price for their wrong actions in a past life or perhaps they're balancing out good and evil in the universe. Still others embrace the idea that suffering is "divine purification" from sins. Some, who think suffering is a test from God, believe it leads to rewards in the afterlife.

But as for Christians, we must look to God's Word (the Christian Bible) for answers. This is where we discover three unchangeable realities:

1. **Pain and Suffering Was <u>Never</u> God's Original Intention.** God is totally holy (Is. 6:3) and His ways are righteous and true (Rev. 15:3). He is intrinsically good and merciful (Ps. 145:8-9). There is no evil in Him (1 John 1:5) nor does He desire that evil people should suffer or die (Ezek. 33:11). Amazingly, the Lord is even kind to ungrateful and evil men (Luke 6:35).

2. **Lucifer's Rebellion in Heaven Is the Origin of All Evil.** It was Lucifer (Not God) that brought evil and chaos to the earth. Long before God created humans, He created angelic beings to freely worship and serve Him in heaven. But in their freedom, one rose up against God to challenge His authority (Is. 14:12-14); Ezek. 28:13-17). His name is known as Lucifer, Satan and the Devil. Thus, there was war in heaven and Lucifer and his angels were cast out of heaven to the earth bringing with them evil and corruption (Rev. 12:1-17). ***That's why we all live in a world of corruption, suffering and death.***

Part II: LIFE Questions

3. **Suffering Is the Direct Consequence of Humankind's Failure in the Garden of Eden.** In the beginning, Adam and Eve were created sinless. But they were free to follow God's righteous purposes or to defy them. God warned them what would happen if they didn't guard themselves against evil (Gen. 2:16-17). But they would not listen! *Thus, the effects of their failure (sin, suffering and death) were intrinsically passed on from them to all their offspring...that includes you and me (Gen. 3:16-19).*

How Then Should We Interpret Life's Sufferings?

1. **God Is NOT Testing Us or Paying Us Back for Our Sins!** That's not His character (James 1:13). God is love and there is no darkness in Him (1 John 1:5; 4:16). He has compassion for those who suffer and comes to our aid when we are tempted (Heb. 2:18). *He constantly reaches to forgive sinners and He never forsakes those who turn to Him (Is. 1:18; Heb. 7:25).*

2. **The Saving Grace of God's Son Brings Forgiveness and Redemption, Yet We Still Live in a Sinful World.** Tragically, our world is corrupted by sin and evil, which causes violence, sickness, disease and death. Salvation doesn't promise a pain-free life...it rescues us from the eternal consequences of sin! Yet, God walks with believers and strengthens us even in the midst of suffering (Ps. 23; 2 Cor. 12:7-10). *That which He doesn't deliver us from, He will deliver us through!*

3. **We Must Have Compassion for the Stricken and Help Those Who Suffer.** People suffer for many reasons: inherited diseases, poor decisions, dreadful illnesses, catastrophic storms, tragic accidents and suffering for the cause of Christ. All of these are the result of a sin-riddled world. *Our assignment is to compassionately help people...not judge them!*

Part II: LIFE Questions

What Does This Answer Really Mean to You?

1. **Never Accuse God or Become Angry with Him for ANY Cause ...Especially Suffering.** As I've said many times, accusing God is like shooting holes in the bottom of your little boat. You'll quickly sink because you're cutting off the ONLY source that can help you! *Trust God, regardless of the outcome and He will walk with you "through the valley of the shadow of death...and you will fear no evil" (Ps. 23:4).*

2. **Don't Confuse "Consequences" of Sin with the Suffering the World Brings.** Suffering caused by foolish actions or decisions is a totally different matter. Violating the laws of society can lead to fines or imprisonment. Ignoring the laws of nature can bring physical harm or even death. *Defying God's laws without repentance has spiritual ramifications that may be eternal!*

3. **If Suffering From the World Comes Your Way, Meet It with Courage, Determination and Faith in God.** Since God didn't cause your suffering, you can fight against diseases and human intimidation knowing the Lord is with you. Be strong in the Lord knowing that He will strengthen you even more (Rom. 5:3-5)!

Thoughts, Ideas or Other Questions to Ponder

Life Question 2

What Happens To People Who Believe in God, But Not in Jesus?

Would a Good God Send Innocent People to Hell?

Tough Question

One person asked, *"What happens to people who die without any knowledge of Jesus or his saving grace?"*

Another had a question about Judaism. He wrote, *"If Jesus died as 'King of Jews,' are Jews accepted in heaven even though they do not accept Jesus but they do accept God?"*

Thinking Deeper

- ✦ Who Is God? What Is Sin? And Do People Even Need Redemption?

- ✦ What About the Jews and Other Religions That Believe in God, But Not in Jesus?

- ✦ Would a Good God Really Send <u>Innocent</u> People to Hell?

Part II: LIFE Questions

Answers Discovered in God's Word

The real questions that should be asked are: *"Who is GOD? What is SIN? And do people even need REDEMPTION?"* Tragically, **"New Age"** thinking has wormed its way into the minds of many...including Christians! It's a mixture of Eastern Mysticism, Hinduism, Pantheism and Paganism. *In this mindset, everything and everyone is a type of "god!"* According to this philosophy, *Sin is simply wrong thinking and acting that can be overcome by personal mediation and self-awareness...along with Progressive Reincarnations!*

When "New Age" is mixed with Christianity, it corrupts sound Biblical doctrine. "Jesus" is replaced by "The Christ Principle" in which there are many "Christs." Redemption is indiscriminately applied to all people. *Therefore there is no need to have "Faith" in order to be "Saved." ALL people, regardless of how EVIL they've lived or what they BELIEVE, are already saved and going to heaven; they just don't know it! Some even believe the Devil will be saved!*

Now, let's clear up all this confused theology, remove the error and discover what GOD says in His word.

What Happens to People Who Die Without Any Knowledge of Jesus or His Saving Grace?

1. **Lack of Knowledge Is NOT a Valid Excuse (Rom. 1:18-23)!** Every person who ever lived has been given an opportunity to respond to some level of God's Light (His Redemptive Truth) concerning who His Son is and what He came to do (John 1:9; Rom. 2:14-16).

2. **If They Respond to Jesus (the True Light of God), More Understanding Will Be Given (Luke 8:16-18).** But those who are old enough to reject God's Light will be judged by the level of Truth they received (John 3:16-21).

What About the Jews and Other Religions That Believe in God, But Not in Jesus?

1. **You Can't Get to Heaven by Believing in God!** Even the demons believe, but it does them no good (James 2:19-20). Only faith (with action) in the Savior, whom God sent, brings salvation (John 3:15-16). *If your "god" is not the Living God who sent His Son, your god is like a dead idol (Ps. 115:4-8)!*

2. **The Jews Believe in God, But They Reject the Savior Whom God Sent to Them (John 1:11-13).** Sure, they had a special covenant with God. But that was the "Old" Covenant which became OBSOLETE when He offered them the "New" Covenant in His Son (Heb. 8:6-13). Yes, Jesus was their "King" (Matt. 27:11). But they rejected Him (Matt. 23:37-39)! *Heaven is theirs...IF they believe in Jesus (Rom. 11:23; John 14:6).*

Would a Good God Really Send Innocent People to Hell?

1. **Wrong Again! There Are NO Innocent People!** All have sinned against God and deserve eternal death (Rom. 3:23; 5:12). That's why God sent His Son...to rescue all who trust in Him (Rom. 5:6-10; 6:23). *However, children who have not reached the age of accountability are assured a place in heaven...forever (Luke 18:16; 1 Cor. 14:20)!* That's God's merciful character.

2. **Yes, God Is Good! And No, Jesus Doesn't SEND Anybody to Hell...They Go There on Their Own!** People who end up in the eternal torment of Hell have to choose to step over the Crucified and Resurrected Savior to get there! *Jesus has done everything possible to rescue them (Rev. 3:20-22)! But if they refused to listen, that's not God's fault.*

Part II: LIFE Questions

What Does This Answer Really Mean to You?

1. **You Make a Grave Error if You Try to Judge God's Character.** God is infinitely Just, yet He is infinitely Merciful. God is Love, yet He sets Righteous Conditions by which men are to be saved. God is Patient, yet He will Judge every person based on their response to His Redemptive Grace in His Son. *Questioning God's character is a vain attempt to place oneself above God!*

2. **Eternal Gratitude Is Your Overriding Response to God Who Showed Mercy Upon You!** When we come to the horrifying reality of how far we stray from the God who loves us, salvation takes on a whole new meaning. We, who deserved no mercy, have been forgiven and adopted as children of God. *For this reason, we give Him our lives and will serve Him forever!*

3. **It Means That God Expects You to Pray for the Lost.** Having been rescued from eternal destruction through no work of your own, you should look with great compassion on those who are as lost as you once were. Pray for them. Reach out to them, not with condemnation, but with God's love. *Show them that if God redeemed you, He can redeem anyone who believes in Him!*

Thoughts, Ideas or Other Questions to Ponder

_____

_____

_____

_____

_____

_____

Life Question 3

Two Questions Concerning the Working of God's Power

Why Won't God Deliver Me From _____?
What About Christians with Alzheimer's Disease?

Tough Question

A Lady Wrote to Me and Asked Two Different Questions:

1. "I have been asking God for deliverance for one particular issue. Since God can do all things, why won't he deliver me?"

2. "If a person has Alzheimer's disease or Dementia and they have already accepted the Lord as their Savior, are they already with the Lord even though they are not dead?"

Thinking Deeper

- ✧ Is There Something About God's Power that I Don't Understand?

- ✧ What Kind of Deliverance Do Most of Us Need?

- ✧ What is the Spiritual Condition of Christians with Alzheimer's Disease?

Part II: LIFE Questions

Answers Discovered in God's Word

Actually, these two questions are more similar than you think. *They both deal with the <u>Power of God</u> and how it works in the lives of Christians.* Let's begin by understanding the basics about God's Power.

Both God's <u>POWER</u> and His <u>WISDOM</u> Work Together ...They Are Limitless (Ps. 147:5)

1. Yes, God Can Do Anything. Nothing Is Too Difficult for Him (Jer. 32:17, 27; Matt. 19:26). God not only <u>spoke</u> the universe into existence, He <u>upholds</u> it with the word of His **Power** (Heb. 1:3). God's purposes will be accomplished and no one can thwart His plans (Job 42:2; Is. 43:13).

2. However, God Never Uses His **Power** Apart From His Infinite **Wisdom**. God knows what's best for you (Is. 48:17 NIV). If He chooses to <u>NOT</u> use His Power the way you want, He has a higher purpose in mind. He only uses His **Power** according to His righteous **Character** and **Purposes** (Rom. 8:28).

But Also, God Gave People Freedom of Choice

1. We Are Free to Obey or Reject God's Will (Deut. 30:19-20). Your choices prove where your heart is (Luke 12:34). If you treasure your relationship with the Lord, you will do what He says (John 14:15).

2. God Is Sovereign, But He Will Not Override Your Freewill Choices (Ps. 81:10-13). Though it grieves the Lord when you walk away from Him, He will not force you to obey His will (Mark 10:17-23).

Part II: LIFE Questions

Now...We Can Address the Two Questions That Were Asked:

1. Why Won't God Deliver Me From (*You Fill in the Blank*)?

   ❖ **It Depends Upon What You Need Deliverance From.** Most of us need deliverance from *Ourselves* ...Not the devil! Our worst enemy is our own Fallen Natures. Since Jesus already delivered us from sin, all we have to do is activate it by seeking Forgiveness and Repenting (changing)! Eph. 4:17-32

   ❖ **If God Chooses to Not Grant Your Request, He'll Give His Grace Instead (2 Cor. 12:7-10)!** God's grace is His **Power** in a different form. Having His strength in your weakness is true **Power**. (Mark 13:9)

2. What Is the Spiritual Condition of Christians with Alzheimer's Disease?

   ❖ **First of All, God's "Keeping Power" Is Absolute (John 10:27-30)!** God knows those who belong to Him and the loss of memory will never change that. Your friend is very secure in Jesus!

   ❖ **But, the Human Spirit Remains in the Body Until the Body Dies (2 Cor. 5:6-8).** God's timing for a saint to be received in Heaven is always perfect (2 Tim. 4:6-8). You may not be aware of this, but the **Lord is at Work** in the hearts of others...even through your friend's illness (Philip. 1:22-24).

Tough Questions You're Afraid to Ask Your Pastor

Part II: LIFE Questions

What Does This Answer Really Mean to You?

1. **You Can Totally Trust Your Life and the Lives of Your Family Members Into God's Loving Hands.** Even if life throws you curves, you are secure with God. God's Power is most evident when we've run out of answers for life's dilemmas and don't know which way to turn. *You can be assured that He will keep you until your course on earth is finished (2 Tim. 4:7-8).*

2. **It's Easier to Blame the Devil for Your Failures Than Yourself!** Let there be no doubt about it...Satan is real and he is more powerful than you are. But, he's also an opportunist. He'll take advantage of your foolishness every chance he can. *So what's the solution? Don't give him that opportunity (Eph. 4:27)!*

3. **Repentance Must Be a Way of Life...Not Just What We Do When We're in Trouble.** The closer you are to God, the more aware you will be when you deviate from His path for your life. *But when you repent (turn away from sin), the power of God is with you to sustain you and keep you from temptation (2 Pet. 2:9).*

Thoughts, Ideas or Other Questions to Ponder

_____

_____

_____

_____

_____

Part II: LIFE Questions

Life Question 4

Same Sex Marriage and Gay Lifestyles

How Should a Christian Respond to These Issues?

Tough Question

"I have a dear friend who is a very respected and skilled professional in Corporate America. He professes to be a Christian and says he loves Jesus with all his heart. *My friend says he is gay and totally accepts his sexual orientation because he believes that was the way God made him.* Since Same Sex Marriage and Homosexuality are taking a center stage in America, how should we, as Christians, view what's going on?"

Thinking Deeper

 ✧ Are Homosexuals Just "Born This Way," or Is Their Lifestyle Really a Sin?

 ✧ Did Jesus Ever Condemn Homosexuality?

 ✧ Is Same Sex Marriage an Acceptable Way of Life?

Part II: LIFE Questions

Answers Discovered in God's Word

First of All, Let's Discover What God and the Bible Are Really All About

1. **The Bible Is the Self-revelation of God.** It tells us who God **Is**, what He **Does** and how the human race got into **Trouble**. But it also tells us about the desire of God and how far He went to **Rescue** all people who trust in Him and His Son, the Lord Jesus Christ (1 Tim. 2:3-6).

2. **Righteousness Can Never Degenerate Down to a List of Do's and Don'ts.** Yes, God has very clear standards for behavior (Gal. 5:19-21). But trying to keep His laws will never achieve true righteousness. Without a living faith in God's Redemptive work, our human works are worthless (Matt. 5:20; Philip. 3:9)!

3. **But, Continuing to Live Outside of God's Standards AFTER Salvation Is Deadly Self-Deception!** God is very clear about this in His word. Take time to read Rom. 6:1-23; Eph. 4:17-32 and 1 John 1:5-10. Many people choose to not believe this, because if they did, they would have to change the way they live!

What Does God and His Word Really Say About Same Sex Unions and Gay Lifestyles?

1. **Are Homosexuals Just "Born This Way," or Is Their Lifestyle Really a Sin?** God's answers are "Yes" and "Yes." God clearly defines sinful behaviors (not just homosexuality) from which we **ALL** need to be redeemed (Rom. 1:18-32; 1 Cor. 6:9-11; 1 Tim. 1:8-11). *ALL people are "Born This Way"...born into every kind of sin that separates us from God (Ps. 51:5; Eph. 2:1-10).*

Part II: LIFE Questions

2. **Did Jesus Ever Condemn Homosexuality?** He didn't have to...God already condemned <u>ALL</u> behaviors contrary to His standards. However, Jesus did approve and confirm God's plan for marriage...a man and a woman (Matt. 19:4-6). *In addition, in John 5:46-47, Jesus endorsed the Law of Moses which included a clear denunciation of homosexuality (Lev. 18:22; 20:13; Deut. 23:17).*

3. **But God Has a Solution for <u>ALL</u> of Us...Regardless of the Kinds of Sins We Are Guilty of.** Redemption is available to <u>ALL</u> who have Faith in God's Son and Repent of their Sins (John 3:15-18; 2 Cor. 7:10). It's as simple as that...IF we believe!

So, How Should a Christian Respond to the Issue of Same Sex Marriage?

1. **Is Same Sex Marriage Acceptable?** The answer is "Yes"...<u>**IF**</u> you **DISREGARD** or **EXPLAIN AWAY** the countless passages in the Bible that oppose <u>ALL</u> behavior outside of God's righteous intentions for people (Isaiah 5:20).

2. **Remember, America Is Not the Kingdom of God...and Neither Are Local Churches!** Do not adopt the standards of Hollywood, Politicians or even Pastors...unless they agree with God's Standards in His word!

3. **But, Be Careful About Judging the Personal Sins of Others (Rom. 2:1-8).** All it takes is <u>ONE</u> Sin (<u>ANY</u> Sin) to separate us from God (James 2:10). If it wasn't for our faith in the Redemptive work of Jesus, we would miss heaven...forever!

4. **Have Great Compassion for <u>ALL</u> Who Live Outside of God's Intentions and Pray for Them.** Don't crusade against one particular sin. Instead, reach out with God's love and befriend the lost (Jude 21-25). *Remember...you were once lost, too!*

Part II: LIFE Questions

What Does This Answer Really Mean to You?

1. **It Means We Can't Live Anyway We Want. Neither Can We Try to Justify Sin According to the Mores of Society.** Some ignore Scripture or claim that it was written by fallible men who claimed to be prophets. Others twist Bible passages and wrench them out of context to justify their lifestyles. Many people look to the entertainment industry as their role models. *But in the end, God has the last word. All people will have to stand before Him to give an account for how they lived.*

2. **It Also Means That You Are Not Superior to Anyone. We All Came From Brokenness!** What a travesty it would be to have been rescued from the pit by God's grace, and then condemn those who are still trapped in sin. That attitude, my friend, invites severe judgment from the Lord (Matt. 18:21-35).

3. **It Means We Serve an Amazing God Who Reached Down to a Fallen World with Love and Redemptive Grace.** Instead of focusing on the sins of others, turn your heart upward. Be eternally grateful to God for His merciful plan of redemption. For without it, <u>YOU</u> would be eternally lost and hopeless!

Thoughts, Ideas or Other Questions to Ponder

Part II: LIFE Questions

Life Question 5

PTSD...Is It a Hopeless Struggle?

Or Is There Purpose Beyond the Pain?

Tough Question

A former member of the military asks this question: "How does a person with PTSD develop and/or maintain faith when the daily struggles that accompany this condition include chronic depression and an overall distorted view of life? *Is there any hope beyond medical and psychological treatment?*"

Thinking Deeper

- ✧ What Is PTSD and Who Becomes Stricken With This Traumatic Disorder?

- ✧ Why Is PTSD So Debilitating?

- ✧ How Can a Person With PTSD Find Purpose Beyond the Pain?

Part II: LIFE Questions

Answers Discovered in God's Word

Post-Traumatic Stress Disorder is not imagined...it's real! I'm not a psychologist, but I know the One who has solutions for ALL human problems. *His name is Jesus...the One who bore the sins and pain of all people. Regardless of their condition or pain, and can come to their aid.* (Is. 53:4-5; Heb. 2:17-18; 4:14-16)

PTSD Isn't Limited to Soldiers Returning From War

- ❖ **It Can Afflict Anyone Who Has Experienced a Life-Changing Traumatic Experience.** It can be caused by any terrifying event such as kidnapping, life-threatening accidents or natural disasters. It's associated with violent physical attacks or even witnessing mass destruction like that of a plane crash or acts of terrorism.

Why PTSD Can Be So Debilitating

1. **It Can Change You Into a Different Person.** According to those who are in the thralls of PTSD, it's an overwhelming emotionally-borne pain. If not controlled through medicine and counseling, it will affect their families and careers. It can manifest itself as heightened irritability, violence, impatience, paranoia and a void that keeps people searching in all the wrong places for solace their entire lives.

2. **Medications Can't Cure the Problem...They Only "Mask" the Symptoms.** Again, according to PTSD patients, many medicines end up contributing to their list of symptoms by adding new ones from side-effects such as headaches, altered personality, increased blood pressure, etc. Unless doctors have personally experienced the ravages of PTSD, they are unable to identify with the patient's struggle, which further aggravates the problem. Patients feel alone and as if no true help is available.

Finding Purpose Beyond the Pain

1. **That's What the Apostle Paul Did.** If anyone should have had PTSD, it was Paul. He was beaten, stoned, left for dead, shipwrecked, betrayed, exposed to the elements and suffered fear, hunger and thirst (2 Cor. 11:24-30). *Yet he viewed his suffering as vicarious in order to help others (2 Cor. 4:8-12).*

2. **That's What GOD Did For You and Me.** Beyond our ability to comprehend, God became flesh and **Volunteered** for a PTSD assignment! He took upon Himself more suffering and pain than we can possibly imagine...even the weight of sin and going to Hell and back for us! Why? Because He loved us (John 3:16-21). When you trust in the Resurrected Christ, He will give you His strength (2 Cor. 12:7-10). *That's called **GRACE**!*

3. **Faith Is Your Lifeline to God's Purpose Beyond the Pain.** Without Faith, you'll never know that God is aware of your suffering and neither will you have access to His Grace. He didn't cause your trauma, but neither did He promise that by being a Christ-follower, you would have a problem-free life. *Therefore, developing and maintaining your faith in God's Son isn't optional...it's essential!* Heb. 11:6 is your undeniable motivation!

4. **Turn Your Pain Into Purpose by Mentoring Others.** God's plan for your life is not derailed by the daily struggles that accompany PTSD. Through God's grace, He can work THROUGH and AROUND the symptoms that plague your life. *Though God may not remove the problems and ailments of PTSD, He promises He will be with you THROUGH them to comfort others just as He has comforted you. (2 Cor. 1:3-7).*

What Does This Answer Really Mean to You?

1. **A Deeper Appreciation Is Due for Those Who Defend Our Country and Are in Harm's Way.** For the men and women who come home from war, a return to life as a civilian can be very stressful. They risked their lives to keep us free, but many times they are neglected, unappreciated...and <u>UNEMPLOYED</u>! *If you see a person in uniform or a former soldier, thank them for their service. If possible, help them in their re-entry process.*

2. **People Who Are Experiencing PTSD Can't Just "Snap Out of It!"** If your friend or a loved one has gone through a traumatic experience, they don't need your sympathy or some homespun psychological remedy. They need your prayers, patience and understanding. It takes trained counsel, time and God's grace to get them through this. *But neither should you be an "enabler" that allows them to persist in self-destructive behavior. Remember, you need professional counseling as well.*

3. **If You Are Suffering From PTSD, Don't Give Up!** At times the stress and pain may become more than you think you can bear. But outside of that prison, there are people who love you dearly and who need your love in return. With God's help, you can break free and live the rest of your life to fulfill His destiny for yourself and those who you love.

Thoughts, Ideas or Other Questions to Ponder

Life Question 6

How Can I Find Meaning In Life?

Who am I? Why am I Here? Where am I Going?

Tough Question

"I know some people who seem to have it all together. They know who they are and where they're going. But not me! I've lived quite a while and done many things, *but I'm still not satisfied with my life. I don't feel like I have any purpose or meaning. What's wrong with me?*"

Thinking Deeper

- ✧ Is There Anyone Else That Feels Like I Do?

- ✧ Where Should I <u>NOT</u> Look To Find Fulfillment?

- ✧ What's the Secret to Discovering True Identity, Meaning, Purpose and Joy in Life?

Part II: LIFE Questions

Answers Discovered in God's Word

First of All, You're Not Alone

One of the richest, wisest and most famous men in the world struggled with this too. His name was King Solomon. *He actually HAD all those things most people think will make them happy, but they couldn't satisfy him.* Here's what he learned that many people never figure out: *He was looking in the wrong places!*

Looking For Fulfillment in All the Wrong Places

1. <u>KNOWLEDGE</u> and Even <u>WISDOM</u> Only Lead to Grief (Eccles. 1:13-18). There's nothing wrong with these...unless you think they can bring you happiness. Here's what Solomon discovered: The more you know, the more it hurts. Why? *Because we can't change people who refuse to change!*

2. <u>PLEASURES</u> and <u>RICHES</u> Only Leave You Wanting More (Eccles. 2:1-11; 5:10-11). This is why the drug user is driven to find a higher high and the wealthy are consumed with accumulating more wealth. They're never satisfied. *"The more you have, the more you want" is what Solomon discovered.*

3. <u>POSSESSIONS</u> and <u>ACCOMPLISHMENTS</u> are Empty Trophies (Eccles. 2:18-23). Why? Because when you die, you can't take them with you. And besides, when you're gone, someone else will inherit all the things you owned. *And if that person is foolish, he or she will <u>waste</u> everything you worked so hard for.*

Part II: LIFE Questions

The Secret to Discovering True Identity, Meaning, Purpose and Joy in Life

1. **Adam and Eve Had It...Then Lost It!** In the beginning, they knew exactly who they were and why God created them. *They were a son and daughter of God, created in His image, blessed, and commissioned to rule over the lower creation in righteousness (Gen. 1:26-28; Luke 3:38).* But they lost it by believing a lie. Since then, all people grope in darkness trying to regain that which was lost (Gen. 3:1-24; Is. 59:10).

2. **King Solomon Finally Came to the Right Conclusion.** Though he struggled trying to find happiness in all the wrong places, he discovered <u>three</u> things that bring meaning to life: *1-Stand in Awe of God; 2-Do What He Says; 3- Don't Try to Hide Anything From Him (Eccles. 12:13-14).* There's nothing that jerks a person out of complacency faster than knowing that we're accountable to God for our lives!

3. **The Apostle Paul Discovered It.** Paul wrote to the Philippians while imprisoned and possibly facing death. Yet, he encouraged others and was unshaken by his predicament. What was his secret that brought meaning to his life? *1-God's Presence Brings Joy; 2-Prayer, Thanksgiving and Thinking on Good Things Brings Peace; 3-Contentment is Being Independent of Outward Circumstances (Philip. 4:4-13).*

4. **So, Who Are You; Why Are You Here; and Where Are You Going?** When you receive God's full redemption in His Son, He restores Identity, Meaning, Purpose and Joy to your life. You are a ***Redeemed Son or Daughter of God***. You have Meaning and Joy because ***You Belong to Him***. You have Purpose because ***God Calls You to Share His Love*** with others who are lost without Him!

Tough Questions You're Afraid to Ask Your Pastor   71

Part II: LIFE Questions

What Does This Answer Really Mean to You?

1. **The Grass Really Isn't Greener on the Other Side of the Fence.** Unfortunately, many people think that another college degree, a new job, a new home, a new car, a new relationship, or a new geographic place to live will make them happy. But if you can actually achieve those "new" things, you'll find that you'll soon run into your same old problem...looking for something <u>NEW</u>! *Without God, fulfillment is like the "pot of gold" at the end of the rainbow. It constantly outdistances you!*

2. **Learn to Embrace What You Have With Gratefulness.** Like the old adage goes, "You don't miss the water till the well runs dry." Live one day at a time enjoying God's creation, His gift of life, and the ones He has placed around you to love and be loved. *Most importantly, enjoy God's immeasurable gift Eternal Life that only comes through His Son.*

3. **Slow Down and Simplify Your Life.** *"But How?"* you may ask. *"My job is stressful and so is my family! I don't even have time for myself!"* True peace is more than a state of mind. It's what your Savior gives you (John 14:27). Then with God's priorities, look at your daily schedule. Reprioritize what's really important and remove self-imposed obligations that will be meaningless in a few days. *Make quiet time with God...even if it's 20 minutes each day.*

Thoughts, Ideas or Other Questions to Ponder

_____

_____

_____

_____

Life Question 7

What Happens to People When They Die?

Are They Just "Sleeping?" Do They "Hang Around?" Or Does Everyone Go Straight to Heaven?

Tough Question

"Recently, the death of a close friend has left me still struggling with the loss. In an attempt to find comfort from the Bible, I read 1 Thess. 4:13-18. According to this passage, people in Christ are "<u>SLEEPING</u>" until the day Jesus returns. I'm not sure I know what that means. If that's true, my image of Heaven just changed. I always thought all of us made a 'Bee-Line' to Heaven when we die. If we don't, then who's up there besides God and the angels?"

Thinking Deeper

- ✧ What Is Life and What Is Death?

- ✧ What Are Some of the Common Misconceptions About People Who Die?

- ✧ So, What Really Happens to People Who Die?

Part II: LIFE Questions

Answers Discovered in God's Word

What Is Life and What Is Death?

All Life originates from God (Gen. 2:7). Life, however, is more than just breathing in and out air. There are three types of Life: Physical, Spiritual and Eternal. In the beginning, God warned humankind that Death would be the consequence of sin (Gen. 2:17). Tragically, sin spread to the entire human race such that all are under the penalty of sin and death (Rom. 5:12). Death is also Physical, Spiritual and Eternal. *Eternal Death is total separation from God, but Eternal Life is found only by trusting the Lord Jesus (John 10:27-28).*

Here Are Some Common <u>Misconceptions</u> About People Who Die:

1. **They're Just "Sleeping."** "Sleep" is a figurative word used in the Bible that describes physical death. It's not like natural sleep that our bodies need. When the Bible speaks of those who are "asleep in Christ," it means *they have entered into His Eternal Rest (Heaven) from all their earthly struggles.*

2. **They "Hang Around" for a While.** The idea that dead people become invisible (ghosts) or change appearances to help (or haunt) those who are still alive, makes for insanely popular Hollywood movies. But that's pure fantasy! *In reality, at the instant of death, everyone stands before the Lord (2 Cor. 5:6-9)!*

3. **They Become "Angels" Who Watch Over Us.** Angels are not transmuted human beings. They are a special creation of spirit beings (prior to people) to carry out God's divine purposes (Gen. 2:1; Heb. 1:5-14; Ps. 103:20). *Angels may appear as humans (Judges 13:3-6), but they are not transformed dead people!*

4. **They Are "Re-incarnated" into Higher or Lower Creatures.** Nowhere in Christianity is there any validity to this concept. This is a pagan reward and punishment ideology based on human performance. *In the Christian Faith, it's our faith in Jesus' perfect obedience, not ours, that makes us acceptable to God.*

So, What Really Happens to People Who Die?

1. **All Who Die Immediately Appear Before the Judgment Seat of Christ.** There is no waiting around in order to finish some type of earthly assignment. And there is no intermediate state of "sleep" or "purgatory." *We are instantaneously transported to God for judgment (Heb. 9:27; 2 Cor. 5:10).*

2. **For Those Who Die Without Christ, There Is No Hope.** God did everything possible to save us from Eternal Death and Punishment. He sent His Son to take our punishment upon Himself and give us His righteousness (2 Cor. 5:15, 21). *That's why all who have rejected Christ will be judged by Him (Matt. 7:22-27).*

3. **Some People Will Never Know...Until It Happens. But Then It's Too Late!** Jesus told a real account of two men. One, named Lazarus, died and was carried to heaven by the angels. The other died and instantly opened his eyes in Hell! *Want a real "Wakeup Call?" Read Luke 16:19-31!*

4. **But Those Who Die In Christ Will Live with Him in Heaven... Forever!** Salvation is not about our personal righteousness or ability to keep God's laws. It's all about our faith in what Jesus did for us. *When we die and stand before God, we will be judged forever "<u>Forgiven</u>" and "<u>Righteous</u>" because of our Faith in Christ!*

Part II: LIFE Questions

What Does This Answer Really Mean to You?

1. Human <u>OPINIONS</u> About Life and Death Are Meaningless. What Really Counts Is What God Says in His Word. Most people fear death. They don't know what will happen to them or if they will "wake up" in a place of torment. Therefore, they concoct theories to help them avoid punishment. Most concepts involve earning paradise by good works. But when they die, they'll face their greatest fear. *Good works can never atone for sin. No one can be saved without Jesus (Acts 4:12).*

2. But for Christians, Death Carries No Fear. God's love through Jesus removes all fears of death and judgment (1 John 4:16-19). This is our ultimate comfort when a Christian friend or loved one dies. *Forever they are with the Lord. All tears are wiped away and there will be no more death, mourning, crying or pain (Rev. 21:4).*

3. It Means You Must Be <u>MOVED</u> with Compassion for Those Who Are Perishing. Compassion is more than just feeling sorry for someone. It means you are "moved" by what you feel and must do something about it. Remember, you are "Christ's Witness" (Acts 1:8) to declare His saving grace to the lost.

Thoughts, Ideas or Other Questions to Ponder

Life Question 8

Are Generational Curses Real?

Should I Be Prayed Over To Break Curses In My Life?

Tough Question

"I've heard some people say there are 'Generational Curses' that follow us throughout our lives. This is disturbing because I've seen evidences of this in my grandparents and parents and I don't want it to happen to me. *Are Generational Curses real? Should I be prayed over to break any of these curses in my life?*"

Thinking Deeper

- ✧ Is There Really Such a Thing as a "Curse?"
- ✧ Does God Punish Children for the Sins of Their Fathers?
- ✧ So, What Really Happens From Generation to Generation?

Part II: LIFE Questions

Answers Discovered in God's Word

Is There Really Such a Thing as a "Curse?"

1. **Some People Think So.** They are convinced that addictions, infidelity, divorce, diseases, bazaar behavior, accidents, premature death and even animal attacks are supernatural curses carried from one generation to the next. Some believe that witch doctors and voodoo priests can place magic spells on people to control their lives.

2. **Yes, Curses Are Real...But They're NOT What You Think!** A Curse is a declaration of harm or torment that befalls someone or something. *The first curse ever uttered was from God against Satan...not against people (Gen. 3:14)!* Tragically, people (and the earth) fell under the curse of punishment for participating in Satan's rebellion (Gen. 3:16-19). *Thus, the only supernatural curse that has any validity or power exists because of sin against God...not from some human utterance against another person.*

3. **But, "THE CURSE" Has Been Broken!** No...it wasn't by some mystic ritual or incantation. We, who were under the curse of being unable to keep God's Law, have been redeemed by God's own Son (Gal. 3:10-14)! *There's no need for a special prayer of deliverance from that which God has already done for you!*

Does God Punish Children for the Sins of Their Fathers?

✧ **Exodus 34:6-7 Has Been Totally Misunderstood by Many!** According to this passage, God *"Visits the iniquity of fathers on the children and on the grandchildren to the third and fourth generations."* "Visit" does not mean that God holds

Part II: LIFE Questions

people accountable for the sins of their foreparents (Deut. 24:16). *Literally, "Visit" means that God "Inspects" and "Observes" each generation to see if they have <u>learned</u> from their parent's failures and have turned from sin to the Lord (Ezek. 18:14-21).*

So, What Really Happens from Generation to Generation?

1. **Tragically, Adam's Sin Has Been Transmitted to All People (Rom. 5:12, 18-19).** Sin is more than wrong words and actions against God, others and even ourselves. Sin is a <u>Spiritual Condition</u> that separates us from God. *We sin because we can't help from sinning. It's part of our fallen nature!*

2. **Biological Tendencies.** Certain susceptibilities, weaknesses and personality traits can be inherited. Diseases, some types of cancers, and addictions can also be passed on from our parents. *That's called life...<u>NOT</u> supernatural curses that have to be broken.* But through prayer and medicine, God can heal!

3. **Sinful Patterns Can Influence Children's Behavior.** Children really do learn what they live. If they live with hostility and abuse, they can become violent. If they live with hatred and immorality, it can shape their souls toward evil. *But if the Lord apprehends their hearts, the cycle of sin can be changed.*

4. **In the Final Analysis, Life-Choices Are Up to You.** There is no scripture that validates Generational Curses. You are not under any supernatural influence (other than sin) to have to repeat your parent's failures. However, if you have opened yourself to the activity of evil spirits, prayer is certainly needed. But don't get caught up in foolish superstitions that play to your fears. *When you accept Jesus as your Savior, you are a New Creature in Christ...Period! (2 Cor. 5:17-21)*

What Does This Answer Really Mean to You?

1. **You Don't Have to Live in Fear.** You have full control over your life to make choices and plan your own future. Don't allow anyone or superstitious ideas to control you or make you live in fear. *In Christ you are truly free (John 8:31-32)!*

2. **But, You Must Be Aware of Generational <u>TENDENCIES</u> in Your Family and Take Positive Steps to Avoid Them.** If you see character traits that are negative...refuse to adopt them! If you see habits that are destructive...break them! If you see health issues that can be inherited...consult with your physician to prevent them from reoccurring in you.

3. **Avoid Involvement With People, Movies, Websites or Books That Engender Superstitions.** As "thrilling" as it may seem to your senses to delve into the spirit realm or play around with Ouija Boards, they can lead to the Occult! That, my friend, is flirting with Satan and evil spirits! *Jesus is the <u>ONLY</u> safe (and righteous) "Door" to the Supernatural World.* When you enter through Him and the work of His Holy Spirit, He will empower you to fight against evil and free those who are held captive by sin and the devil (Luke 4:18-19; Matt. 12:28)!

Thoughts, Ideas or Other Questions to Ponder

Life Question 9

Paralyzed by Tough Decisions?

How Should Christians Make Good Life-Choices?

Tough Question

"Our family is facing a tough life-decision that will affect where we live, the kind of work we do and our entire family. We're torn knowing that our choices will deeply impact every aspect of our lives. *Do you have any criteria that we can use to help us with this decision? Also, we want to teach our children these concepts as they grow up.*"

Thinking Deeper

- ✧ Freedom of Choice...Is It a Blessing or Your Worst Nightmare?

- ✧ What Are Some Biblical Principles For Making Good Life-Decisions?

- ✧ How Can You Know If You're About to Make a Wrong Decision?

Part II: LIFE Questions

Answers Discovered in God's Word

Freedom of Choice Is a Gift from God

Freedom of Choice is a blessing...but it can turn into your worst nightmare! It's like when God gave Adam and Eve the freedom to choose from <u>ANY</u> tree in the garden (Gen. 2:16). Their wrong choice was devastating! *But even though decisions are <u>YOURS</u> to make, God will not leave you without His counsel (Ps. 32:7-9).*

Biblical Criteria for Making Good Life-Decisions

1. **Put All Options on the Table. Ask God for Options You Haven't Thought of Yet.**
   - ✧ *Don't act on partial information.* Research all options. (1 Sam. 16:1-13)
   - ✧ *Don't think that every open door is from God.* Examine it closely. (Prov. 14:12; 1 Thess. 5:21)
   - ✧ *Don't "Just follow your heart" or move on impulse...*your heart may be wrong (Prov. 4:23; Jer. 17:9)
   - ✧ *Don't do anything without asking God for His wisdom.* (Prov. 3:5-6; James 1:5-8)

2. **Evaluate Each Option**
   - ✧ *Look at the Big Picture...*the way God sees you and His ultimate purpose for your life. (Jer. 29:11-13)
   - ✧ *Look at your Goals* (Prov. 29:18). What should this decision ultimately produce? (Is. 32:15-18)
   - ✧ *Look for the Obvious.* It's usually hidden behind your opinions and emotions. (Matt. 13:14-16)
   - ✧ *Look for the Simple.* God reveals Himself in the simple truths of life. (1 Cor. 1:27-29)
   - ✧ *Look for Biblical Principles and the Ways of God...*they transcend your emotions. (Is. 55:8-9)

- ❖ *Look into the Future.* Project each option ten years into the future. What would be the possible outcome of each (negatively or positively)? Will it bear the fruit of wisdom? (James 3:17-18)

3. **Seek Outside Counsel**
   - ❖ *Listen to Yourself.* Step outside of your personal biases and objectively listen to your own words. You may be able to correct yourself before you make a mistake. (1 Cor. 11:31)

   - ❖ *Listen to Eldership.* Watch how they express concern over the decision you're about to make. Also, listen carefully to what is <u>NOT</u> said as well as to what <u>IS</u> said! (Prov. 18:17)

   - ❖ *Listen to the Still Small Voice Within You.* Don't violate that Voice. It's usually God's Spirit trying to keep you from the heartache and pain of a wrong decision. (Is. 48:17-19 NIV)

Now, Here's a Self-Test to Determine if You're About to Make a Wrong Decision

1. Do I want something so bad that I can't wait?

2. Am I afraid to seek counsel because they might tell me something I don't want to hear?

3. Is the deal I'm about to enter into too good to be true? *(There are always hidden costs!)*

4. I don't care what happens tomorrow. I want to enjoy this now!

5. I'll just go ahead and do it! It's easier to ask for forgiveness than to ask for permission.

6. Am I willing to ignore Biblical principles or Prophetic warnings in order to satisfy my heart's desire?

Part II: LIFE Questions

What Does This Answer Really Mean to You?

1. **Success in Life Is All About Making the Right Choices.** Every major life decision you make leads to a certain outcome, either positive or negative. The detailed list above may seem a bit excessive, but life is too important to make foolish decisions that may be irreversible (Prov. 14:12).

2. **But Even if You Have Made a Wrong Choice in Life, God Can Help You.** Only God has the power to turn evil into good by changing the final outcome of a foolish decision. That doesn't mean that you won't suffer the consequences, but the Lord can teach you a lesson you'll never forget or repeat again. Then, after you've been forgiven and restored, you can help others to not repeat your failure (Ps. 51; Luke 22:31-34) Thus, you will be a witness of God's mercy and grace that you didn't deserve.

3. **Your Life Experiences, Both Successes and Failures, Can Be Turned Into Wisdom for the Next Generation.** That's the role of eldership. You've lived long enough, seen many things, and know what makes for good and poor decisions. If you don't warn the next generation of life's pitfalls, they're bound to fall into them. If you don't point the way to God and His Light, they'll lose their way in darkness (Ps. 78:6-8).

Thoughts, Ideas or Other Questions to Ponder

Life Question 10

Why Didn't God Answer My Prayers?

I Prayed to God...But He Didn't Help Me.

Tough Question

"I live in another country where jobs are very difficult to find. Unfortunately, I made a terrible mistake at work, but I admitted it and asked my supervisors to forgive me. I am a Christian, so I prayed and accepted my fault in front of God. I spoke to Him and said, 'I am sorry for my mistake, please forgive me and let me keep my job.' But my supervisor asked me to resign. ***Why didn't God help me when I prayed? I feel so helpless!***"

Thinking Deeper

- ✧ Is God Obligated to Answer a Heart-Felt Prayer?

- ✧ What Are Some of the Ways That God Answers Prayer?

- ✧ What Should You Do If God Doesn't Answer Your Prayers in the Way You Want?

Part II: LIFE Questions

Answers Discovered in God's Word

Life Is Fragile and Very Unforgiving

"Life Isn't Fair, But God Is Good!" That was the book that Robert Schuller wrote when he accidentally bumped his head and had to undergo brain surgery. Nature is unmerciful when storms, floods and wild fires hit without warning. *And companies have rules that if you break them, there are no second chances.*

God Hears and Answers Prayers...But Only According to What's <u>BEST</u> for You

1. **Prayer Is Not Magic and God Is Not a Genie.** There is nothing "automatic" about God. Just because people pray doesn't mean that He is obligated to grant their every desire. God weighs each request that we make based on what's best for us and in keeping with the appropriate season of our lives (Is. 48:17 NIV; 1 Pet. 5:6-7).

2. **God Hears Prayers of Repentance and Answers Those Who Call Upon Him.** The Lord is aware of you and your sufferings (Ex. 3:7). He has compassion for you (Matt. 9:36) and has not forgotten you (Heb. 6:10-12). It is always God's kind intention to answer your prayers (Mark 1:40-42; Heb. 4:15-16).

3. **But When God Answers Prayers, It's According to <u>HIS</u> Wisdom...Not Ours (Is. 55:8-9).**

    ✧ God's Answer May Be, "<u>YES</u>." *"I've heard your prayers, your heart is right, the need is genuine and I will do this for you because it will bless you and further My cause on earth."* (1 Kings 3:7-14)

Part II: LIFE Questions

- ✧ **Other Times God Says, "NO."** *"The thing that you're asking for is not good for you or for others. If I gave you what you're asking for, it will cause more difficulty later on. I have something better for you now. And besides that, I'm protecting you from dangers that you're not aware of."* (Acts 16:5-10; Ps. 91:11-16).

- ✧ **Or, God May Say, "MAYBE."** *"I want to do this for you, but there are some things you must learn. You have to suffer the consequences of your failure. If you handle this with humility, then I can bless you in a different way. I can mightily use you to help others."* (Ps. 51:9-13; 2 Cor. 1:3-4)

- ✧ **God Can Also Say, "YES...BUT NOT NOW."** *"The timing isn't right for you to receive this request now. Neither you nor others are ready for it. But in the meanwhile, I will give you My Grace so that you will be able to endure your difficulties with My strength."* (2 Cor. 12:7-10)

- ✧ But I thought Jesus said, *"If you ask Me **ANYTHING** in My name, I will do it."* (John 14:14). Look at the context of this passage. It's about representing Christ in the world...not your personal desires.

What Should You Do If God Doesn't Answer Your Prayers in the Way You Want?

1. **Never Accuse God or Become Angry with Him.** Accusing God of wrongdoing is like shooting holes in the bottom of your little boat. Thank Him for loving you so much that He didn't grant a request that wasn't the best for everyone involved. ***Whatever He keeps you from is for your good (Job 22:21-22).***

Part II: LIFE Questions

2. **Trust God and Follow Him No Matter What (Dan. 3:17-18).** If God says "No," ask Him for other options (Prov. 16:3, 9). Build up your faith in His word; encourage yourself in the Lord; help others; and do what God calls you to do. ***In due season you will reap good things...if you don't give up (Gal. 6:8-9).***

What Does This Answer Really Mean to You?

1. **It Means That You Are Completely Secure With God.** Security comes from knowing that the Lord will guard you from anything that may bring harm to you or others...even misdirected prayers.

2. **It Would Be a Good Idea to Listen to Your Own Prayers.** This will help you pray with maturity. If you recognize that you're praying a selfish prayer, you can change your request so that it's more in keeping with the kind of prayers that God answers.

3. **You Can Help Others Who May Be Struggling With This Issue.** Now that you've gained insight into how God answers prayers, you can share it with others. It's amazing how spiritual truth brings clarity to confused minds...if their hearts are open.

Thoughts, Ideas or Other Questions to Ponder

Part III: Questions and Problems Concerning <u>Church</u> and <u>Ministry</u>

These questions are perhaps the most delicate of all. The reason is because they deal with sensitive issues that affect our belief system, trust in leadership, and why and where we attend church. Church splits have erupted over these complex issues and pastors have been removed from office. *That's why it's essential that we answer these questions from the objectivity of God's word rather than from longstanding traditions or emotional opinions.*

Again, I am indebted to the questions sent to me from those who I've ministered to across the years and who continue to follow our ministry. I'm especially grateful to fellow pastors who have submitted questions that they know need biblically honest answers. *I've also drawn from heart-wrenching personal experiences in ministry that I, along with my colleagues, have grappled with to find the mind of the Lord as revealed in His written word.*

Given the controversial nature of these questions, I ask that before you accept or reject the answers I give, carefully read the Scriptural references. One of my favorite passages comes from the account of the Bereans in Acts 17:11 – *"Now these were more noble-minded than those in Thessalonica, for they received the word with great eagerness, <u>examining the Scriptures daily to see whether these things were so.</u>"*

Part III: CHURCH and MINISTRY Questions

Thoughts, Ideas or Other Questions to Ponder

Church and Ministry Question 1

Do All Religions Lead to God?

Does God Care Which Faith I Choose to Follow As Long as I Believe in a Higher Being?

Tough Question

"I'm a young 'Millennial Generation' person who is much more open minded than my 'Boomer' parents. I don't stumble over gay or bi-sexual lifestyles. What people choose to do with their lives is up to them. *I'm sure there's some higher power that guides our lives, but I honestly don't care which one it is. I know you're a Christian pastor, but don't you think all religions lead to God?*"

Thinking Deeper

- ✧ Why Do All People Intrinsically Worship a God?

- ✧ How Do Other Belief Systems Try to Lead You to God?

- ✧ What's Different About Christianity? How Does It Show You the Way to God?

Part III: CHURCH and MINISTRY Questions

Answers Discovered in God's Word

Yes, You Are Very Correct. All Religions Lead to What Some People *Think* Is "God."

Among all people or tribes on earth, there is an obvious universal phenomenon to worship a deity or a philosophy of life. Their god may be a stone idol, an impersonal force in nature, a plurality of deities, an ideology, or the Creator of the universe. Therefore, there must be a Supreme Being who instills within people a strong desire to know and worship Him. *But is there only One True God? And is there only One Way to Reach Him?*

Let's Look Briefly at Some Other Beliefs to See How They Try to Lead You to God

1. The Buddhist Way to God. Actually, Buddha never believed in the existence of any god. But his followers worship his "enlightened" philosophy. Their goal of life is to escape pain and suffering by right thinking, thus extinguishing all human desires and achieving "non-existence of self." If you don't achieve it before you die, then you are reincarnated until you do. *So, my friend, is this the kind of "god" you want to follow?*

2. Can Islam Lead You to God? Its founder, Muhammad, taught that Allah is the one true all-knowing, good and merciful God. *But He cannot be known.* Since they have very, very strict laws for living, Allah judges you based on your ability to obey and balance between good and bad deeds. *So, if you think you can be perfect enough to earn their Allah's approval, try it. But the consequences of failure are severe!*

3. Now, Let's Look at Judaism. For the Orthodox Jew, their God is similar to that of Christians. But they have a problem of how to deal with sin and receive forgiveness from the Lord. In the Old

Part III: CHURCH and MINISTRY Questions

Testament, the law required the death of animals as substitutes for the consequences of sin. But they stopped animal sacrifices in 70AD! *So, do you think you can earn God's favor by obeying <u>ALL</u> His laws? If you fail, then all you can do is to hope He will forgive you if you <u>TRY</u> to repent and do good deeds.*

4. **Want to Try <u>Christian Science</u>, <u>Scientology</u> or <u>New Age</u>?** God is an impersonal force or principle of life, truth, love, intelligence, and spirit. <u>Everyone is a type of god</u> with unlimited powers over their own universe. Death isn't real. You are reincarnated until you reach oneness with their <u>impersonal</u> God! Salvation is doing good things to offset the bad and being reborn into self-awareness. *Is this the kind of God you want to worship?*

Now, Let's Look at Christianity. It's Not a Religion...It's a Personal <u>RELATIONSHIP</u> with the Living God!

1. **Our God Isn't a Dead Founder of a Religion...He's the Living and Awesome God that Created All Things.** We believe in one God who exists as three Persons...Father, Son and Holy Spirit. Jesus Christ is God, the Son, who became flesh, died for your sins, was resurrected and rescues all who have faith in Him.

2. **We're Not Trying to "Find" God...He Reveals Himself to Us!** Finite and sinful people cannot comprehend or approach an infinite and holy God. Therefore, our God became a human being to make Himself known, remove the sin that separates us from Him, and restore us back to Himself.

3. **Our God Loves You so Much that He Personally Paid the Penalty of Your Sins and Gave You His Righteousness.** No other religion offers you that! It's impossible to gain forgiveness by trying to keep a set of laws. The only way to salvation and eternal life is to believe in what God's Son did <u>FOR</u> you that you could not do for yourself (Eph. 2:8-10).

Tough Questions You're Afraid to Ask Your Pastor

Part III: CHURCH and MINISTRY Questions

So, Do You Think All Religions Lead to the <u>Same</u> God? Sure, they offer moral and philosophical ideas about God. But only in Christ do you have a True Savior. He's the <u>only way</u> that you can be restored to a Personal <u>Relationship</u> with God. *Eternal Redemption (that you can't earn and don't deserve) is only through His Son, Jesus.*

What Does This Answer Really Mean to You?

1. **This Is the Same Crisis That Adam and Eve Faced.** The battle in the Garden was over the word of God. Satan's declaration was that what God had said wasn't true (Gen. 3:1-5). Since then, false religions have sprung up throughout the earth drawing people away from the one True and Living God and his word.

2. **So, It Really <u>DOES</u> Matter What You Believe and Who You Believe In.** Your eternal state of existence depends upon what you believe. To fail to believe in the Redemptive work of Jesus is to miss out on Eternal Life. God cares so much about what you believe that He personally came to the earth to show you the <u>ONLY</u> way to the Father (John 14:6; Acts 4:12).

3. **Therefore, You Must Guard Your Mind and Heart From Worldly Ideologies and Religions That Draw You Away from the Living God.** It's easier to be lead astray than you think. That's why Jesus warned us about deception (Matt. 24:5, 23-25). That's also why the Apostle Paul gave similar warnings (2 Cor. 11:3-4).

Thoughts, Ideas or Other Questions to Ponder

Church and Ministry Question 2

How Can I Share My Faith With Unbelievers?

*How Can I Minister to Atheists
Or People Who Mock God?*

Tough Question

One person wrote in to ask **If**, **When**, or **How** to share her faith with an unbelieving friend whose husband (also an unbeliever) is in the hospital, on a ventilator and slipping in and out of consciousness.

Another person asked, "What is the best path to take when trying to minister to atheists or people (including family and friends) who think nothing of mocking God?"

Thinking Deeper

- ✧ What Things Should You Absolutely **NOT** Do?

- ✧ What Does God Say in His Word About the **RIGHT** Way to Share Your Faith With Unbelievers?

- ✧ But What Happens if People Reject Your Witness for Christ?

Part III: CHURCH and MINISTRY Questions

Answers Discovered in God's Word

First of all, Here Are Some Obvious Things You Should NOT Do

1. Don't run in with guns blazing trying to win the heathens to the Lord. Unfortunately, many well-meaning zealous Christians end up scaring people away from God. *Just start by being a friend!*

2. Don't quote scripture thinking they'll get convicted, fall on their knees and get saved. You'll just run them off. *Besides that, nobody likes a hard sell!*

3. Don't try the "Turn or Burn" threat. *Using Hell to scare people into become Christians won't last.* God never uses fear to redeem people...He draws them to Himself with LOVE! True salvation is being "Born Again" (John 3:3-8). This is a spiritual change from the inside out. God transforms your human spirit, redeems your soul and restores you to Himself.

4. Don't make promises that God will do something He may not do. For instance, don't say, *"God will heal your husband if you have faith in Jesus."* ***Eternal Salvation is not to be equated with temporary physical healing.*** (Sure, God heals...but you can't use this as bait to lure people into salvation.)

5. Since Jesus calls His followers the "light of the world," don't be so afraid of sharing your faith that you hide your light under a basket (Matt. 5:13-16). *Remember, God commands us to go into the unbelieving world and make disciples for Christ (John 17:14-18; Matt. 28:18-20).*

Now, Let's Go to God's Word to Learn How You Should Share Your Faith

1. **Sharing Your Faith Is More Than What You <u>DO</u>...It's About Who You <u>ARE</u> and Who <u>LIVES</u> within You!** You can't "save" anybody! That's the work of the Holy Spirit (Titus 3:3-7). If you try to talk people into believing in Jesus, then someone else can talk them out of it! You are the Redeemed of the Lord with the power of the Holy Spirit living in you (Acts 1:8). *It is <u>He</u> who leads you in what to say and do (Matt. 10:18-20).*

2. **Remember, "One Size" <u>DOESN'T</u> Fit All!** Every person's journey through life is different. Make sure your approach is seasoned with grace and that it fits the unbeliever's particular situation (Col. 4:3-6). Many have been hardened by life's disappointments. Even if they are belligerent in their unbelief, continue praying for them. *Your mission is not Confrontation... it's <u>Compassion</u> (2 Tim. 2:23-26).*

3. **You Must *"Always Be <u>READY</u> to Give an Answer"* for Your Faith (1 Pet. 3:14-16).** Being "ready" is more than just memorizing a bunch of scriptures to share with people. It means that you have an ongoing personal relationship with the Lord Jesus and have "sanctified Him in your heart." *It means that your life is an <u>example</u> to unbelievers of how Christians live.* Then when you speak, they'll believe you.

4. **Finally, If People <u>REJECT</u> Your Witness...It's Between Them and God.** Only the Holy Spirit can change lives. Salvation isn't Behavior Modification; it's a Total New Nature! *That only happens when people <u>RESPOND</u> to the work of the Holy Spirit through you (that's called freedom of will).* Remember, some people even rejected Jesus, Himself (Mark 6:1-6; Matt. 19:16-22; John 6:70-71)!

Part III: CHURCH and MINISTRY Questions

What Does This Answer Really Mean to You?

1. **Witnessing for Christ Doesn't Have to Be Complicated.** You don't have to earn a theology degree and neither do you have to be an extrovert. If you just quietly **live** what you believe, others will take notice. Then, if they ask why you have confidence when others are fearful or are falling apart, you can simply say, *"The Lord is my strength." It's as simple as that!*

2. **But, You Must Be Aware of People and the World Around You.** If you see someone who is grieving, comfort them. If you know people are in trouble, pray for them in the quietness of your heart. If you see injustice, ask the Lord to correct that which is wrong...*even if He chooses to work through you.*

3. **It Means That You Know God Is Working Through You... Even If You Don't See Any Results.** You never know who is watching you or what impact your life will have on others. What you do (or don't do) is being noticed, even if you don't realize it. *The Lord can cause others to remember your actions and quiet words (even years later) and bring them to Christ.*

Thoughts, Ideas or Other Questions to Ponder

Church and Ministry Question 3

Can Women Serve as Leaders And Pastors in Church?

What About the Apostle Paul's Writings in 1 Tim. 2:9-15?

Tough Question

> "Most churches will concede that there is ample evidence for women to operate in ministry...*as long as they are under the covering of male leadership.* But women are limited to teaching other women and children. However, they are also allowed to evangelize, witness for Christ, use spiritual gifts, prophesy and help serve in many other capacities. *But, is there any clear scriptural support for Christian women to be in Governmental Positions over men in the church (e.g., Pastors, Elders, Bishops, or Apostles)?*"

Thinking Deeper

- ✧ What Are the Common Arguments Against Women Serving as Leaders in the Church?

- ✧ What Did God Say in His Word About the Relationship Between Men and Women?

- ✧ What Then Shall We Do?

Part III: CHURCH and MINISTRY Questions

Answers Discovered in God's Word

What Are the Common Arguments Against Women Serving as Leaders in the Church?

1. **Men Claim That Eve Disqualified Both Herself and <u>ALL</u> Women.** They like to point to Gen. 3:16 and say that God commanded women to be ruled over by men. BUT...that was <u>NOT</u> a command of God. He simply stated the tragic result of sin. *Remember, Adam's sin was just as bad as Eve's. He caved in to temptation as well! According to Scripture, it was <u>Adam</u> that brought sin upon the entire human race! (Rom. 5:12-14)*

2. **Men Quote 1 Tim. 2:9-15 in Which the Apostle Paul Refused to Allow Women to Teach or Have Authority Over Men.** There were two things that Paul was addressing in this passage:

   1) He was speaking to a ***particular problem*** in the local church in Ephesus...not to <u>ALL</u> women in general! Apparently they were patterning themselves after pagan women who were publically sensual and outspoken. This had to be corrected.

   2) Paul was also addressing a very ***prejudiced cultural world*** in which women held low social positions and were prohibited from being trained in the scriptures. Knowing that redeemed attitudes between men and women could not happen overnight, Paul set an orderly structure over the ***authority struggles*** between men and women, bringing stability to both the church and the home (1 Cor. 11:3-16; 14:34-35). He directed women to <u>LEARN</u> rather than try to exercise authority in the church (1 Tim. 2:11). *Had Paul tried to abruptly reverse that social order, it would have caused utter chaos (1 Cori. 3:1-3).*

What Did God Say in His Word About the Relationship Between Men and Women?

1. **Before Sin Entered Humankind, Men and Women Were Equal in Authority.** God commissioned <u>BOTH</u> Adam and Eve to rule together (Gen. 1:28). In their <u>pre-fall</u> relationship, they had equal access to God without competition, power struggles or abuse of authority. *Created uniquely in God's image, they ruled Eden with interdependence...inseparably committed to one another and the Lord (Gen. 2:23-24).*

2. **In Redemption, God Removed <u>ALL</u> Barriers...Including Gender Prejudice (Gal. 3:28).** Sin is the basis of quarrels, envy and striving for superiority (James 4:1-3). In redemption, both men and women honor one another according to the gifting of God in them (Eph. 5:21-33). *Through redemption, men and women are reunited to their original mission as <u>co-rulers</u> over the earth.*

3. **Are There Biblical Examples of Women in Leadership Roles?** This was rare because of social prejudices. However, **Deborah** was a **Prophetess** called by God to Judge Israel (Judg. 4:4-10). **Priscilla** (whose name was mentioned before her husband's) brought **Doctrinal Correction** to Apollos (Acts 18:18, 24-26). And the early church had **Women Prophets** (Acts 21:9) **and Deaconesses** (Tim. 3:8-11; Rom. 16:1-2).

What Then Shall We Do?

1. **Return to the <u>Pre-Fall</u> Biblical Model with Redeemed Attitudes.** Both men and women must lay aside fallen attitudes (Eph. 4:22-25) and allow their paradigm to be renewed according to God's original design. *God does not show partiality (Acts 10:34). The Lord does <u>NOT</u> discriminate against women!*

Part III: CHURCH and MINISTRY Questions

2. **Evaluate Leadership Gifts Based on the Righteous Fruit of God's Call.** God redeems, calls, anoints and distributes gifts to whom He decides (1 Cor. 12:11-27), not according to male or female gender. *Submission is not on the basis of "inferior" or "superior." We submit to the Gifts and Callings in people, regardless of whether they are men or women.*

What Does This Answer Really Mean to You?

1. **Unfortunately, Social Prejudices Still Plague the Church...Even After 2,000 Years!** This must change! We must lay aside all injustices. This includes racial, cultural, social, financial, and gender prejudices. *God's church must be prejudice free!*

2. **We ALL Must Reevaluate Our Personal Prejudicial Attitudes.** This includes BOTH men and women! Because of the social mores of the past, some women may still believe they don't have the right (or calling) to operate in leadership roles in God's church. *This also must change!*

3. **If You Are a Male Pastor or Church Leader, You Must Lead the Way.** A male-dominated leadership paradigm is NOT a Biblical example of Redemption! Pastors and Eldership must remove all prejudices and recognize leadership gifts regardless of whether they reside in men or women.

Thoughts, Ideas or Other Questions to Ponder

_____

_____

_____

_____

Church and Ministry Question 4

If I'm Not Fulfilled at My Church, Is It Okay to Leave?

Do I Have to Wait for God to Release Me?

Tough Question

"I've been told by my friends that if I leave my church, I would be 'fair game' for the devil. They said that if God brought me to this church, I can't leave until He tells me to go. Yet, I don't feel fulfilled where I am and I want to find a new church. ***Why can't I leave anytime I want?***"

Thinking Deeper

- ✧ What Is "Church Membership?"

- ✧ Why Do People Want to Leave Their Local Churches?

- ✧ So, Is There a Right Way To Leave a Church?

Part III: CHURCH and MINISTRY Questions

Answers Discovered in God's Word

Here's a Deeper Question: "What Is Church Membership?"

1. **You Don't "Join" God's Church...You're "Born" Into It!** The Church of the Lord Jesus Christ is much more than a local fellowship. It's God's "Called-Out Ones" (ekklesia). We're called <u>OUT OF</u> Darkness and <u>INTO</u> His marvelous Light (1 Peter 2:9). When you are "Born Again" by God's Spirit, you have entered His Kingdom (John 3:1-8) and have become a member of Jesus' Church in the world (Matt. 16:15-19).

2. **A Local Church Is "<u>A</u>" Geographic Expression of Jesus' Church...But It's Not the <u>ONLY</u> Church on Earth!** The early church was much different than today. There may have been only one Christian fellowship for hundreds of miles. Today, we have many different expressions of culture, worship and preaching styles in the same city. *There is nothing in scripture that says you can't attend a local church of your choosing.*

Why Do People Want to Leave Their Local Churches? *(This is certainly not an exhaustive list.)*

1. **Geographic Relocation.** This is a very legitimate reason to leave and join another church. The local church really should be "local" so that Christians can actively engage in the life of that fellowship.

2. **Offenses.** Offenses against other Christians are the <u>*worst possible reasons*</u> to leave a church. The only proper solution is to repent, forgive and restore the relationship (Eph. 4:31-32; Col. 3:12-16).

Part III: CHURCH and MINISTRY Questions

3. **Personal Failure.** Some people, who have had moral failures, become too embarrassed to remain in the same church where they are known. Unfortunately, they walk away and seek a fresh start in a new church. But God has a better way for everyone involved to handle personal failure (Gal. 6:1-2; 1 John 1:9).

4. **The Pastor.** There's nothing wrong with liking a certain pastor... as long as your faith in God doesn't fall apart if the pastor has a moral failure or leaves the church (1 Cor. 1:10-13; 3:4-9). But if a pastor sins and hasn't truly repented, or if he deviates from Biblical truth, that is certainly justification for leaving and finding another church (1 Tim. 5:17-21; 1 John 4:1-3).

5. **Desiring Different Expressions of Worship and Places to Serve.** The Lord knows we have different personalities and gifts. There's nothing wrong in finding a church where you are comfortable and can volunteer to serve. Wherever you attend, be faithful (Heb. 10:23-25) and serve well (Rom. 12:1-8).

So, Is There a Right Way to Leave a Church?
The Answer is "YES!"

1. **The Responsibilities of a Person Who Is Considering Leaving:**
   ✧ Open your heart to your pastor. If at all possible, resolve any problems and remain where you are.
   ✧ If you must leave, don't leave Jesus' Church! Diligently find another local church to attend.
   ✧ Make sure disillusionment isn't becoming a pattern. Don't restlessly wander from church to church.
   ✧ If you decide to leave, ask for a Letter of Transfer to the next church. This shows good and honest intentions.

2. **The Responsibilities of the Pastor and Congregation:**
   ✧ If people choose to leave, release them to their destinies in Christ. Remember, they're God's "sheep," not yours!

Part III: CHURCH and MINISTRY Questions

- ❖ No guilt-trips and no control! They are <u>NOT</u> leaving God simply by leaving your local church.
- ❖ Never use them as examples of people who betrayed you and walked away from your ministry!
- ❖ Pray for them and genuinely ask for God's Blessings over their lives as they move on.

What Does This Answer Really Mean to You?

1. **Your Personal Relationship with the Lord Is of Upmost Importance.** Don't let anything or anybody cause you to walk away from God's Church. If you're not regularly attending another fellowship within a few weeks after you leave your church, *your faith will begin to grow weaker* (Heb. 10:23-25).

2. **Refuse to Be Placed on a Guilt-Trip by <u>ANYONE</u>!** God never places guilt on people. Jesus came to forgive our sins and remove our guilt (Ps. 32:5; 1 John 4:10). *Nowhere in the Bible does it say we can't choose a church of our liking.*

3. **But, Be Careful About Becoming Too Picky.** Sometimes we can become so opinionated and particular that nothing will satisfy us. Make sure this isn't happening to you. *There are no "perfect" churches or congregations anywhere on earth!*

Thoughts, Ideas or Other Questions to Ponder

Part III: CHURCH and MINISTRY Questions

Church and Ministry Question 5

Will God Continue to Bless Me Even if I Don't Tithe?

What If I Decide to Not Go to Church at all?

Tough Question

"I've always enjoyed going to church...except for one thing: They're always asking for money! At times I think they want my money more than me! Some are **casual** about asking me to give. But others **plead** for money, drawing on my sympathies for their financial burdens. And some make me feel that if I don't tithe, I'm in jeopardy of **losing out** with God. *It makes me not even want to go to church.* So, will God continue to bless me even if I don't tithe?"

Thinking Deeper

- ✧ What Is Tithing and Why Should We Give Tithes and Offerings?

- ✧ What Is Church Attendance All About?

- ✧ So, Will God Continue to Bless Me Even if I Don't Tithe or Go to Church?

Tough Questions You're Afraid to Ask Your Pastor   107

Part III: CHURCH and MINISTRY Questions

Answers Discovered in God's Word

What Is Tithing and Why Should We Give Tithes and Offerings?

1. **God Wants Our Hearts...Not Our Money!** But here's the problem: our hearts are tied to our possessions and money. The way we spend our money indicates where our hearts are (Matt. 6:21). Money and things are like false gods...they can draw our hearts away from the Lord (Matt. 6:24). Tithing means giving a tenth of all to God (Gen. 14:20). *When God is **FIRST** in your life, you'll honor Him with your income. This invokes God's blessings over everything else that you have (Prov. 3:9-10).*

2. **In Reality, We Don't "Give" Tithes...We "Return" Them Back to God.** The air we breathe, the water we drink, the food we eat, the ability to make money (even our very souls) belong to God. Therefore, the tithe really belongs to the Lord, not to us (Lev. 27:30). Offerings are our free-will giving beyond our tithe. *Giving money to the work of the Lord on earth is an act of gratitude for all His provisions.* If we withhold tithes and offerings, the Bible says we're stealing from God (Mal. 3:8-9)!

3. **Actually, Tithing Benefits Us More Than Our Churches.** Yes, God intends for the tithe to support those who minister to you (Num. 18:23-24). *But the spiritual blessing you receive far outweighs your financial gift (Mal. 3:10-12).* Don't assume that tithing is just an Old Testament law. Though it's not emphasized in the New Testament, it doesn't negate your requirement to honor God and support His work financially with your tithes and offerings.

What Is Church Attendance All About?

1. **Attending Church Isn't a Religious Obligation...It's a Spiritual Refueling Station.** God meets with His people when they gather to seek His will (Matt. 18:20). In His presence, all fears are resolved and His blessings are forever (Ps. 21:6; 31:20; Jude 24). When we gather to hear God's word preached and taught, our faith is refueled (Rom. 10:14-17). *When we gather with believers, our lives are enriched (Heb. 10:24-25).*

2. **Don't Let Disillusionment with the Local Church Keep You from God's Kind Intentions.** Offenses with church members can make people want to run away. This can especially be true if church leadership disappoints you. Learn to forgive people and overcome offenses (Prov. 19:11; Col. 3:13). *Believers belong to God's family (Eph. 2:19) and it pleases Him when the family gets together (Acts 2:42-47).*

So, Will God Continue to Bless Me Even if I Don't Tithe or Go to Church?

1. **God's Blessings Are Always Conditional.** Every spiritual blessing that God has to offer can only be received when we respond to Him in Faith and Covenant (Ex. 19:4-6; Heb. 11:1-6). Unless we meet God's righteous requirements, even forgiveness and salvation is withheld (Matt. 6:14-15; Mark 16:16).

2. **What Happens If I Don't Tithe?** God's love is unconditional and can never be earned. Neither can salvation be purchased or lost based on money (Eph. 2:8-10). *But refusing to tithe is failing to show gratitude for your salvation. Therefore, God is under no obligation to fulfill His promise in Mal. 3:10-12.*

Part III: CHURCH and MINISTRY Questions

3. **What Happens If I Don't Go to Church?** If you're saved, God will not take away your salvation if you stop attending church. But if you **ARE** saved, you will **WANT** to gather with the redeemed community. *If you don't, then you'll miss out on God's blessings that He gives through His Church (1 Cor. 12).*

What Does This Answer Really Mean to You?

1. **It Means You Must Never Get Tight-Fisted With God!** The Lord has freely given to you what you could never earn on your own...Eternal Life! He sent His Son to die for your sins and to give you His righteousness...which is impossible for you to achieve by your conduct. Therefore, you owe Him more than tithes and offerings. *You owe Him your very soul!*

2. **You Should View Your Money Differently.** If you want to see where your heart is, just look at your checkbook! If you've left God out of your finances, you've left Him out of your life!

3. **Never Operate with a** *"How Little Can I Do and Still Be Accepted by God"* **Attitude.** That's a recipe for disaster! You can fool your family, your pastor or even yourself. But you can't fool the Lord! God sees the motives of your heart and He will reward you accordingly.

Thoughts, Ideas or Other Questions to Ponder

_____

_____

_____

_____

Church and Ministry Question 6

Why Do Some Pastors Have Thousands of Followers While Others Only a Hundred or Less?

Are Smaller Churches Less Important Than Larger Ones?

Tough Question

"The pastor of our church recently left to take a much larger church in the nearby city. Though it made us all sad, I can understand why he would want the prestige of pastoring thousands rather than a couple hundred. But I'm wondering why he didn't just stay here and build up our church? Is it God's will for pastors to leave like this? *Does this mean that our smaller church is less important than larger ones?*"

Thinking Deeper

- ✧ What Does God's Word Say to Congregations Concerning This?

- ✧ What Does God's Word Say to Pastors?

- ✧ What Is "Success" in God's Eyes?

Part III: CHURCH and MINISTRY Questions

Answers Discovered in God's Word

What Does God's WORD Say to Church Members?

1. **Exalting Preachers Isn't a New Problem.** Paul had to deal strongly with this in the early church (1 Cor. 1:11-17; 3:3-9). Former Gentiles followed Paul; the philosophical minded followed the eloquent preaching of Apollos; converted Jews followed Peter; and another group rejected all human leaders claiming, "Christ Only!" They got their eyes off Jesus and began to compare preachers! *It's alright to prefer certain preaching styles...as long as your faith is in the Lord Jesus and not in the preacher!*

2. **God Sees His Church Differently Than We Do.** Church size (large or small) doesn't impress God...but maturity does! All people (including pastors) have different abilities and gifts to "do business" for the Lord. As in Matt. 25:15, God gives "quantities" according to abilities. Some have natural skills to creatively lead the masses, while others have a personal touch to nurture smaller numbers. Some are called to travel <u>and</u> pastor a church at the same time. *All of these are valid pastoring gifts... <u>IF</u> they bring maturity to the Body of Christ.*

What Does God's WORD Say to Pastors?

1. **Congregations Are Not Stepping Stones to Larger Ministries.** It's one thing for your Denomination to change your assignment when they recognize where your gift is best suited. But it's a totally different dynamic to "lobby" for a bigger church. *We must guard ourselves from Pharisaical pride. All of us who are called to minister should read Matthew 23 one more time. It's a sober reminder of what <u>Not</u> to do!*

Part III: CHURCH and MINISTRY Questions

2. **Stay Within the "Sphere" of Ministry That God Has Assigned to You (2 Cor. 10:13-16).** Jesus gives gifts, calls leaders, and sets them in His Church according to how they function best (Eph. 4:7-16). *The grace that He gives to minister to the needs of the few is just as valid as the grace to minister to the masses.*

3. **Be at Peace With Who You Are and the Gifts God Has Given You.** Ambition is great...as long as it motivates you to use your God-given gifts to their fullest. Remember, we who pastor are but "links" in God's chain that connect people to Him. *Don't under or over-estimate the power of who you are.*

Here's the Real Question: "What Is <u>SUCCESS</u> in God's Eyes?"

1. **Is the Pastor of a Mega-Church More Successful Than the Pastor of Less Than a Hundred?** Jesus preferred the term "Great" rather than "Successful." According to Him, the one who <u>SERVES</u> others is Greater (Matt. 20:20-28). *Greatness is determined by the hearts of the pastors, not the size of their churches.*

2. **The World Sees Success as "Bigger, Better, Faster" than their Competition.** As God matures His gifts in people, He can enlarge the "sphere" of their assignment. But it comes with a price (Matt. 20:21-23). *Neither pastors nor their churches should compare themselves with others (2 Cor. 10:12-13).*

3. **God Sees Greatness as <u>INTEGRITY</u> and <u>FAITHFULNESS</u>!** In the parable of the talents, God rewarded the "5-talent" servant the same as the "2-talent" servant (Matt. 25:14-23). Both were faithful over the gift given to them. Jesus only had **Twelve** disciples. And Ananias is credited with only **One** act of ministry ...praying for Saul who became the Apostle Paul! (Acts 9:10-20). *Now, who would doubt their Greatness?!*

Part III: CHURCH and MINISTRY Questions

What Does This Answer Really Mean to You?

1. **The Church Belongs to Jesus, Not to Pastors or Church Members.** Jesus is the Head of His Church and it is He who loves her, gave Himself up for her, sanctifies her, and prepares her for heaven (Eph. 5:23-27). Eldership is charged to oversee (not own) the local church and be examples to the flock (1 Peter 5:1-4). Parishioners are required to follow godly leaders and cooperate with their Biblical governance (Heb. 13:17).

2. **For Those of Us Who Pastor, It's Not About US...It's About GOD and His PEOPLE.** By God's grace, His Son gifts us to function in His Church as Apostles, Prophets, Evangelists, Pastors and Teachers for the purpose of equipping and maturing GOD'S PEOPLE (Eph. 4:7-16). *Our focus should be on how much God loves THEM...not on our special gifting (Ps. 78:70-72).*

3. **Honor God's Gift in Leadership...But Be Careful You Don't Slip Into Unintentional Idolatry.** There's nothing wrong with being grateful and showing appreciation to the pastors or elders who lead and guide your church. But to place them on pedestals invites disappointment. Leaders are ordinary people with extraordinary callings. We need God's grace, forgiveness and restoration just like the people we serve. *If your faith falls apart if your pastor fails or leaves, you're in trouble!*

Thoughts, Ideas or Other Questions to Ponder

Church and Ministry Question 7

When Your Pastor Sins!

What Should Your Church Do?

Tough Question

"I've read of these things happening in other churches...but never in my church. When the unthinkable happened, all I wanted to do was run away and pretend it didn't. The pastor that we all dearly love has failed morally and the scandal is the lead story in the evening news. *What are we going to do?*"

Thinking Deeper

- ✧ What's the First Thing That Should Be Done?

- ✧ Should Local Churches Try to Handle This Problem by Themselves?

- ✧ What's the Primary Goal in Dealing With this Difficult Issue?

Part III: CHURCH and MINISTRY Questions

Answers Discovered in God's Word

To Begin With...There Are No Quick or Easy Solutions!

This problem is far too complex to adequately handle in a brief teaching like this. The lives of human beings and their spiritual futures, both in and out of the pulpit, are at stake. However, there are some Biblical Principles in God's Word that give wise counsel and godly guidance. *Unfortunately, the tendency is to go to the extremes...either too harsh or too lenient. Neither of these reflects the Wisdom of God.*

As Mentioned Before, Pastors Are Ordinary People with Extraordinary Callings and Requirements.

Those of us who are called to the ordained ministry are not immune to the human problem and our fallen natures. We need God's grace and forgiveness as much as our congregation. However, God's call on our lives requires us to be **examples** to the flock of God as we follow Christ (1 Cor. 11:1; 1 Pet. 5:1-3). This most specifically includes our speech, conduct, love, faith and moral purity (1 Tim. 4:12). *For this reason, we must guard ourselves from becoming a disgrace to the cause of Christ (1 Tim. 3:1-7).*

How Then Should a Church Deal with a Pastor Who Sins?

1. **First of All, Get the Story Straight!** Many a pastor's life and ministry have been destroyed by a false accusation. And many a congregation has been destroyed by a pastor that has no accountability. The church elders must discover what's true and what isn't. This most certainly involves personal meetings with the pastor and everyone involved (Matt. 18:15-17). *Never make a judgment based on a single accusation (1 Tim. 5:19).*

Part III: CHURCH and MINISTRY Questions

2. **God Really Does Have Standards for Conduct (Ex. 20:1-17; Eph. 4:17–5:13; Gal. 5:16-26).** Though no one is able to live a sinless life, there can be no acceptable justification for purposefully setting aside God's Standards...regardless of their position in the church (1 Tim. 5:19-21). *This is called accountability!*

3. **Seek the Counsel of Seasoned Eldership Outside Your Church.** Emotions run high during this kind of crisis. It ranges from lynch mob mentalities to "heroizing" the pastor for remaining strong during a failure. *Without the Biblical counsel of eldership outside of your church that you <u>trust</u>, you can easily err in judgment (Prov. 11:14).*

4. **There Is No Substitute for a Repentant Heart.** God clearly sets forth in scripture the following evidences that lead to forgiveness and restoration: <u>Faith</u> in Christ's redemptive work (Gal. 2:20); Recognizing and <u>acknowledging sin</u> (1 John 1:7-9); <u>Godly sorrow</u> and humility that leads to repentance (2 Cor. 7:9-10); <u>Repentance</u>, which is turning from sin and toward God (Acts 26:18); <u>Renouncing</u> and resisting sin (Eph. 4:20-32); <u>Seeking forgiveness</u> and forgiving others (Matt. 6:12-15); and <u>Accepting God's reconciliation</u> and living as one who has been fully reconciled to God (Col. 1:21-23; Jude 24-25). *If this doesn't happen, the consequences are severe (1 Tim. 5:20)!*

5. **The Primary Goal Is <u>RESTORATION</u>...Not Punishment.** Restoration carries the idea of a physician mending a broken bone. In all cases, it must be done in a spirit of gentleness and not with malice (Gal. 6:1). *However, there are natural consequences that accompany sin.* At times, a pastor may need professional counseling to resolve habitual problems. If total trust is lost by the congregation, the pastor may be unable to remain in his church. Above all, forgive and pray for your pastor and his family. If at all possible, he should be fully

Part III: CHURCH and MINISTRY Questions

restored to his position in ministry. *If God can restore the vilest of sinners, can He not forgive and restore an erring pastor?* (Read Zech. 3:1-7 to see how God restores leaders.)

What Does This Answer Really Mean to You?

1. **Sin Is Not a Light Matter...For the Clergy or Laity.** Sin destroys lives, families, ministries and careers. A casual, *"I'm sorry...now let's move on,"* will never remove the horrifying results of sinful actions. It takes the Blood of our Savior to forgive and restore a person back to fellowship with God and his fellow man. *Yes, God is merciful, but Redemption cost Him the death of His Son!*

2. **But Neither Should a Person Wallow in Sin, Remorse, Self-Pity and Self-Condemnation.** Once true repentance, forgiveness and restoration have taken place, the matter is closed with God (Ps. 32:1-5; 103:8-14). Whether you are the one who sinned or the one who was sinned against, *forgiveness and restoration is your only option* (Matt. 6:14-15; 18:21-35; Gal. 6:1-2).

3. **We're All on This Amazing Journey with God Together.** There are none who are righteous and none who will ever walk through life without sin (Rom. 3:23-24). We all are in desperate need of the Savior...whether we are church leaders or church members. *So, let's do this with love, gentleness, compassion and forgiveness in our hearts toward one another (Col. 3:12-14).*

Thoughts, Ideas or Other Questions to Ponder

_____
_____
_____
_____

Part III: CHURCH and MINISTRY Questions

Church and Ministry Question 8

What Happens to Aging And Retired Pastors?

Are They "Pastor Emeritus" or "Pastor Superfluous?"

Tough Question

"Our beloved pastor, who is 66 years old, has recently retired after serving as our senior pastor for over 30 years. Our new pastor is wonderful, but we still miss the man who we trusted for three decades. *When we asked him what he will be doing, his response was a bit vague.* On his last Sunday with the church, they named him 'Pastor Emeritus.' *So, what do aging pastors do after they retire or leave a church?"*

Thinking Deeper

- ✥ What Does God's Word Say About Your Ministry When You Advance In Years?

- ✥ What Are Some Practical Suggestions for Pastors to Consider?

- ✥ What Should Younger Pastors Do...<u>BEFORE</u> They Get Old?

Part III: CHURCH and MINISTRY Questions

Answers Discovered in God's Word

What Does God's Word Say About Your Ministry When You Advance in Years?

1. **At the Right Time, Choose a Successor to Continue God's Work.** Moses chose Joshua; Elijah anointed Elisha; and Paul trained Timothy and Titus. God is trans-generational (Ps. 90:1-2). He continues His work by transferring His mantle of anointing and authority to the next generation (2 Kings 2:9-15).

2. **You May Be "Emeritus," but You Are Definitely NOT "Superfluous!"** Emeritus is an honorary title indicating what people _used to be_...before they were put out to pasture! *But Elders in the Lord's work function as Elders for LIFE* (Deut. 34:7; Ps. 92:14-15; Acts 20:24; Philem. 8-9; 1 Pet.5:1-3; 2 John 1).

3. **Never Stop Declaring God's Strength and Power...Regardless of Your Age (Ps. 71:17-18).** You are an example for all to see that the calling and power of God does not diminish with age. The older you are, the more you are _honored for your experience, knowledge and wisdom_ (Lev. 19:32; Prov. 16:31).

4. **Warn the Next Generation About Mixture with World Religions (Josh. 23:2, 6-8).** As Joshua did when he was advanced in years, so *elders must guard the flock of God* against the winds of doctrine and the trickery of men that draw people away from the Lord (Eph. 4:11-16; Acts 20:28-30).

5. **Speak Prophetically Over Your Children and Grandchildren (Gen. 48:10-20; Heb. 11:21).** This certainly includes your *spiritual children* as well (1 Tim. 1:2, 18; Titus 1:4). Unless they know who they are in God, they can miss their destinies. Speak it and record it as their heritage in the Lord.

In Addition, Here Are Some Practical Suggestions for Pastors to Consider

1. **"Called" Pastors Don't Retire...But They Do Change Gears!** The ministry is not a career choice...it's a divine calling. Stay ministry minded and take advantage of your new season. Enjoy family and life. *Re-tool, Re-fire and Re-invent yourself with new methods of ministry, including Internet technology.*

2. **Redirect Your Self-Esteem.** A change in seasons requires a change in goals and purpose. Most pastors realize it's difficult to remain in the same church with their successors. When your successor takes over, you're no longer the chief shepherd of your local church. *New purpose comes from your next assignment in God.*

3. **Transition from Management to Mentoring.** The loss of authority, recognition and regular preaching can produce grief and demise of purpose. Stay alive in God's word and trust Him for your future (Is. 46:3-4). The assignment of the older generation is to pass on their wisdom and experience to younger leaders (Mal. 4:6). *Ministry to the masses transitions into personal impartation (1 Thess. 2:8)!*

4. **Remember, <u>YOUNG</u> Pastors, One Day You Will Be <u>OLD</u>!** Absolutely, trust God for your future, but also plan for <u>STREAMS</u> of income other than your church retirement. In order to not live in poverty after your working years, you'll need Social Security, 401K's, Investments or perhaps rental property. And Don't Forget Health Insurance! *Be as wise with your future finances as you are with caring for souls and overseeing your church (Prov. 6:6-8; 30:25).*

Part III: CHURCH and MINISTRY Questions

What Does This Answer Really Mean to You?

1. **This Is Another Reason Why You Should Give Tithes and Offerings.** Your giving provides for the many ministry needs of your church. But don't forget that this also includes retirement benefits for your pastors, who gave their entire lives caring for you and opening the truth of Scripture to your heart. *They are worthy of your continued financial support (1 Tim. 5:17-18).*

2. **If You Are a Church Administrator or Ruling Elder, Don't Fail to Provide Some Type of Retirement for Your Pastor.** Tragically, I've seen pastors who worked for "peanuts" their entire lives, and all they received when they retired was a celebration dinner. Set up a 401K or some other type of fund that earns income for this specific purpose. If you are part of a denomination, be sure this is in place. *God honors those who care for His servants (Matt. 10:41-42)!*

3. **Pastors, Your Life's Work Will Never Be Forgotten...By the Lord or Those You Serve.** The years of godly service, countless hours spent preparing sermons and teachings, counseling appointments beyond measure, tears shed over people's losses, and joys shared for their successes, are written on the hearts of those that you have ministered to (2 Cor. 3:2-3). And the Lord, who called you into His service, is not so unjust as to forget your loving ministry to His people (Heb. 6:10). *He will reward you, both in this life and in Heaven (2 Tim. 4:7-8)!*

Thoughts, Ideas or Other Questions to Ponder

Church and Ministry Question 9

Disqualified From Church Membership!

Should Pastors Ever Turn People Away from Church?

Tough Question

"My question has to do with *Restoration*. As a compassionate pastor, I am committed to the Biblical mandate to 'Restore those who are caught in sin...in a spirit of gentleness' (Gal. 6:1). But what about those who join the church, live in open sin, draw others into their sin, ignore godly counsel, leave the church and then want to return? *Should we accept everyone who wants to be part of us, or is there a reason to turn some away?*"

Thinking Deeper

- ✧ What Does "Spiritual Restoration" Mean?

- ✧ How Do We Know if a Person Is Progressing Toward Restoration?

- ✧ Should Some People Ever Be Turned Away From the Church?

Part III: CHURCH and MINISTRY Questions

Answers Discovered in God's Word

First of All, Restoration Is the Very Heart of God

1. **Spiritual Restoration Is the Renewing of a Fallen World and People Back to God and His Purposes.** It's the amazing story of how God reverses evil caused by Lucifer's angelic insurrection in heaven that brought his dark and corrupt kingdom to the earth (Gen. 1:2; Rev. 12:7-9).

2. **"Light" Is God's Power That Brings Restoration.** God's first act of restoration was when He commanded Light to overcome the spiritual darkness that had come to the earth (Gen. 1:3-4; John 1:4-5; 2 Cor. 4:6).

3. **When We Receive God's Light, Our Restoration Process Has Begun.** When humanity failed to represent God's authority in the earth and take dominion over evil, we forfeited our divine purpose (Gen. 1:26-28; 3:1-24). *But in the Light of God's Son, our Destiny is restored again (Acts. 26:18; Philip. 2:15).*

But...Spiritual Restoration Is <u>VERY</u> Conditional!

1. **Salvation Is Freely Offered...But Not Without Conditions!** Unless a person **Believes** (trusts) in Christ's redemptive work (Mark 16:16) and **Bears the Fruit** of salvation (Matt. 7:17-27), God's saving grace has not been fully received. *Without salvation, we do not have the Light of God in us (John 8:12).*

2. **People Who Reject God's Light Have Rejected God's Restoration!** God's Light is made available to all people by the Truth of His Word (Ps. 119:105, 130; 2 Tim. 3:15-17). But those who "love" darkness have chosen to remain blinded to the Light of Salvation by their unbelief (John 3:18-21; 2 Cor. 4:3-6).

Part III: CHURCH and MINISTRY Questions

3. **By This We Will Know if People Are Progressing Toward Restoration Back to God and His Church**

    ✧ **They have Faith** in the Person of Jesus Christ and His redemptive work. (Rom. 5:1-2; Gal. 2:20)

    ✧ **They Recognize and Acknowledge Their Sins.** (Ps. 32:1-5; 1 John 1:7-9)

    ✧ **They Have Godly Sorrow and Humility** that leads to repentance. (2 Chron. 7:14; 2 Cor. 7:9-10)

    ✧ **They Are Repentant**, which is turning from sin and toward God. (Acts 2:38; 3:19; 26:20)

    ✧ **They Renounce and Resist Sin.** (Eph. 4:20-32; Col. 3:5-10)

    ✧ **They Seek Forgiveness and Forgive Others.** (Ps. 51; Matt. 6:12-15)

    ✧ **They Accept God's Reconciliation and Live as Those Who Have Been Fully Redeemed.** (Rom. 5:10; 2 Cor. 5:18-21; Col. 1:21-23; Jude 24-25)

What Then Shall We Do?

1. **So, Should Some People Be Turned Away From the Church?** Unconditional Love is **not** unconditional <u>TRUST</u>. Trust must be earned. If there is **<u>No True Repentance</u>** and if they become **<u>Predators</u>**, pastors have every right to turn away "Light-Rejecters." (Matt. 18:15-17; Acts 20:28-31; 1 Cor. 5:1-13; 1 Tim. 1:19-20).

2. **But, Never Stop Praying for the Lost!** Deep in your heart, pray and continue to reach out with God's compassion for even the vilest of sinners. Who knows what God might do (2 Tim. 2:24-26; Jude 22-23).

Part III: CHURCH and MINISTRY Questions

What Does This Answer Really Mean to You?

1. **Freedom of Will Is a Frightening Reality!** As much as we want everybody to be saved and go to heaven, it just won't happen! Why? Because God gave every human being the freedom to determine their own destiny...whether is agrees with God's plan of redemption or not. *Even Jesus said, "Many are invited but few are chosen" (Matt. 22:14 NIV)...meaning they would not respond to God's invitation for redemption.*

2. **Don't Feel Guilty When People Refuse to Be Restored.** Even Jesus couldn't restore everyone He spoke to! The rich young ruler walked away from Him (Matt. 19:16-23) and Judas rejected His warning in the upper room (Matt. 26:21-25). *Try as you may, some just refuse to be made whole!*

3. **But You Have to Try!** Matthew 28:18-20 is called the Great "<u>Commission</u>"...Not the Great "<u>Option</u>!" Jesus commanded us to "Go" and "Proclaim" the Gospel knowing that some will never believe (Mark 16:15-16). *But if you never Go or Proclaim, then some will never hear and be saved (Rom. 10:14-16)!*

Thoughts, Ideas or Other Questions to Ponder

Church and Ministry Question 10

Betrayals and Offenses Among Christians

How Should We Handle Them?

Tough Question

"I've never been so hurt in all my life! A friend in my own church betrayed me! The hurt was beyond what I could bear and I'm not sure what to do. Part of me wants to confront this person, but another part just wants to leave the church and start over again. *I know I should forgive, but I don't know how."*

Thinking Deeper

- ✧ What Should I <u>NEVER</u> Do About an Offense?

- ✧ How Does God Want Me to Handle Offenses?

- ✧ How Can I Get Healed From an Offense?

Part III: CHURCH and MINISTRY Questions

Answers Discovered in God's Word

Unfortunately, Offenses Are Part of Life

All of us are imperfect human beings prone to sin. We sin against God by breaking His laws and we sin against ourselves by shameful actions for which we are condemned. But many times we offend and hurt others...some of whom we love and attend church with. *Since it's inevitable that we will either offend or be offended, we must know how God's wants us to handle it when it happens.*

How Can I Deal With an Offense?

1. **Whatever You Do in <u>ANGER</u> Will Be Wrong!** To do nothing makes a hurt fester. But to lash out with anger makes it worse (James 1:20). <u>*Never try to deal with an offense when you're angry!*</u> Humility, regardless of who's at fault, brings healing (Ps. 51:17).

2. **Step <u>AWAY FROM</u> and Rise <u>ABOVE</u> the Offense.** It's essential to separate an offense from the one who caused it (whether you were offended or caused an offense). Remember, God hates sin, but He loves the sinner (Rom. 5:8)! *Love is higher!*

3. **Remember How <u>GOD</u> Deals With <u>Your</u> Sins and It Will Soften Your Heart (Ps. 103:10-14).** If God forgave you of much, how can you hold a grudge against another (Matt. 18:21-35)? With a softened heart, you may choose to speak with the offender, or just forgive them and let it go. If it was you that hurt someone, confess your sin to them and seek forgiveness. *Forgiveness is a miracle...it heals hearts and restores lives.*

How Can You Get Healed From an Offense?

Many years ago a visiting pastor spoke at the church where I served for 30 years and brought a remarkable message on how to

Part III: CHURCH and MINISTRY Questions

deal with offenses. If you follow these steps, God will not only **heal** you but He can also **reverse** the offense.

1. **Don't CURSE the Offender.** This is true whether the offender is someone else or if it is you! To wish evil upon someone who hurt you or to retaliate against them is totally rejecting the way of Christ (Luke 6:35-36). *To wallow in self-condemnation for hurting someone will never solve the problem.*

2. **Don't REHEARSE the Offense.** To rehearse the details of an offence over and over is like consuming your own regurgitation! It will sicken you! It's a never-ending cycle of replaying the scene, wishing you had done something differently. *You can't change the past, but God has a new beginning for you...if you are willing (Is. 43:18-19).*

3. **Don't NURSE the Offense.** This is like a young mother who holds her newborn baby close to her and feeds it from her own body. When you nurse an offense, you are feeding the hurt and keeping it alive! *If you do this, anger (or remorse) will take on a life of its own and consume you (Ps. 37:8)!*

4. **But, DISPERSE the Offense with Love and Forgiveness.** Dispersing an offense is like pouring a barrel of toxic poison in the middle of the ocean. It will be so diluted that it is no longer toxic. *If you have God's love and forgiveness in you, the venom of offenses and hurts will be removed (Ps. 103:12).*

5. **Then God Can REVERSE the Offense!** If you follow these steps, God can turn evil into good (Gen. 50:20). He can heal estranged hearts and mend broken relationships. You can learn lessons you'll never forget. *Even if the person you offended doesn't forgive you, God does...if your heart is right!*

Part III: CHURCH and MINISTRY Questions

What Does This Answer Really Mean to You?

1. **An Offense Is More About <u>YOU</u> Than the Person Who Offends You!** All offenses begin in the mind...how you process an offensive word or action. Therefore, a test of your character is how you choose to respond and recover from an offense. *To feed an offense brings disdain, but to overlook an offense brings glory to you (Prov. 19:11).*

2. **Offenses Are Stumbling Blocks to Spiritual Growth.** We can become offended about many things...some great and some very insignificant. Regardless of what caused them, holding offenses will sidetrack your destiny and keep you from forgiving your brothers or sisters in Christ (Matt. 5:23-24; 2 Tim. 2:23-24). Guard your heart against offenses. *But most importantly, ask the Lord to help you from being an offense to others...regardless of what the situation might be (Luke 17:1; Rom. 14:19-21).*

3. **When You Stop an Offense <u>BEFORE</u> It Gets Started, You've Done a Great Favor to Yourself and to Others.** Offenses begin like a trickling leak in a dam. If it isn't plugged immediately, it becomes a great flood that destroys many lives (Prov. 17:13-14). *It's better to <u>STOP</u> it than to suffer the consequences.*

Thoughts, Ideas or Other Questions to Ponder

130　　　　　*Tough Questions You're Afraid to Ask Your Pastor*

EPILOGUE

Discovering God's Answers for Yourself

As I've mentioned earlier, one of my favorite New Testament passages comes from the account of the Bereans in Acts 17:11 - *"Now these were more noble-minded than those in Thessalonica, for they received the word with great eagerness, <u>examining the Scriptures daily to see whether these things were so.</u>"*

It's one thing to hear a persuasive sermon or teaching and believe it's true because of the eloquence of the speaker or the agreement of the congregation. But it's a totally different matter to personally search the Scriptures to make certain that what you hear really is God's Truth. I'm not talking about being skeptical or having a basic mistrust of preachers. **But unless you make truth you own, you'll always refer to someone else's words rather than to God's Word.** And so it is with seeking to discover answers for the many questions or dilemmas that arise in your life. Search them out for yourself! *If it's not confirmed by God's written word, don't believe it!*

I'm certain that many of you have questions that were not covered in this book. Therefore, I've added this Epilogue to assist you in your quest. If you actually follow the next steps, you'll be amazed at how rich your walk with the Lord will become.

EPILOGUE – Discovering God's Answers for Yourself

How Can You Discover Answers for Yourself in God's Word?

1. **Begin Building a Personal Bible Reference Library**

   Bible References are guides that help you understand what the Bible is saying, what certain words mean and how you can look up key information. The basic Bible References include:

   - **A "Study Bible."** This is a Bible with helpful information about each book of the Bible. It also includes Bible Verse Cross References. They point to similar passages that give added dimensions of understanding. When selecting a Study Bible, choose a version that's easy for you to read and understand.

   - **A Concordance.** This is a handy tool to help you look up and find where certain words in the Bible are located.

   - **A Bible Commentary.** Commentaries give a verse by verse explanation of what each passage in the Bible means.

   - **A Bible Dictionary.** It's important to know what words in the Bible mean and who important people are in the Bible.

   - **An English Dictionary.** Don't forget this resource. It gives added depth to the meanings of English words you read.

2. **Set Aside Study Time Each Week**

   You can do this a little each day, or schedule an entire morning or evening...whatever works best for you. The main idea is consistency. Blend reading with study so that you know what you're reading. If you read a word or a passage you don't understand...look it up in your Commentary and Dictionaries. You'll be surprised at how much insight you'll gain!

EPILOGUE – Discovering God's Answers for Yourself

3. Understand the Big Picture...God's Overall Intention

The Word of God is all about **Restoration**. It's how God redeems and restores fallen people and a corrupt world back to Himself (John 20:31; Luke 19:10; Acts 3:18-20). It helps you to discover God's **Character**, your **Identity** and how to fulfill His **Assignment** for you on the earth (2 Tim. 3:15-17).

4. Develop an Orderly Way of Thinking...Ask Key Questions and Pay Attention to Details

- ✧ Let's say you're interested in a specific topic...like raising children, a personal issue you're struggling with, or an area that involves a major decision you're facing.
1) Look up key words about the topic in your Bible Concordance; 2) Write down the scriptures that you believe would shed some light on the issue; 3) Find and read those scriptures in your Bible. *For proper context, be sure to read the passages above and below the one you've found.*

- ✧ Use Your "Study Bible" to Discover What a Scripture Means in its Proper Context.
Who was the author and why was this particular book written? What was happening in the life of the author? What is the chapter or paragraph emphasizing? Who's talking to who and why? What was the "present crisis" when this passage was written and who were the people it was addressed to? *Without proper context, you can easily misinterpret and misapply God's Word!*

- ✧ What Does the Rest of Scripture and Bible Scholars Say About This Passage?
Look up the cross references in the side margins of your Bible. Follow the trails through Scripture and let Scripture explain itself. Don't exclude passages that you may not understand or agree with. *Read what proven Christian scholars (past and present) have written about the passage.*

EPILOGUE – Discovering God's Answers for Yourself

5. Discover Spiritual Principles that Transcend Time and Culture

Spiritual Principles are **Spiritual Laws** (like sowing and reaping), God's **Character** and His **Purposes**, Patterns of **God's Ways** for you to follow, Patterns of **man's Failures** for you to avoid, and **Promises** from God that can be received only through obedience and covenant with Him.

6. Application, Application, Application! *(Me First, then Others—1 Cor. 9:27)*

Ask yourself how Bible passages address your needs and inspire you toward your potential. How do they help you to negotiate the storms in your life and give you solutions and hope for your dilemmas? *How do they motivate you to grow in faith, serve God and reach your destiny in Christ?*

7. Finally, Plan Ahead! Find What God Has Said BEFORE You Make Major Decisions

Life is made up of the choices and decisions you make. They determine the road you take, the quality of your life and the final destination where you end up. If you violate the Principles found in God's word, you'll end up lost and destroyed! Why? Because God knows what's BEST for you and He warns you in His word when you begin to get off course (Is. 48:17-19 NIV). *The more familiar you are with God's word, the less likely you are to end up at the wrong destination in life.*

Other Books Written
By Dan Rhodes

My prayer is that this book has been a blessing to you as you seek for answers to life's perplexing questions. When you delve into God's written word, the Holy Spirit will help you to better understand His righteous character and loving purpose for your life...especially in the midst of personal dilemmas. May the Lord continue to richly bless you, give you His wisdom, and lead you in His everlasting way.

I invite you to visit our Destiny Navigators website to review some of the other books and postings that are made available to you and your loved ones. *www.DestinyNavigators.org*

Setting Your Heart on the Kingdom

A 12-Book Series for an Entire Year - Daily devotional teachings from every book of the Bible. Principles of the Kingdom of God are surfaced with practical applications for life.

Navigating the Uncharted Waters of Your Destiny

A Workbook Study Guide Series - Helping people discover and live in their God-called destiny. After each teaching section is a personal workspace for you to write answers to key questions asked.

Navigating Life With God's Compass

A Spiritual Navigational Guide - Biblical Teachings taken from each of the 66 books in the Bible with practical Life-Navigational insights to help you avoid the pitfalls of life and lead you to your destiny in Him.

Other Books Written by Dan Rhodes

Pursuing God's Kingdom Above All Else

A Workbook Study Guide - A "fill-in-the-blank" teaching manual on the Kingdom of God with practical life-application assignments. Since this workbook is designed to be taught in study groups, it is available in both Teacher and Student Editions.

Once Upon A Kingdom

The Epic Story of God's Kingdom - It's the amazing account of Good and Evil, Human Destiny and God's Eternal Purposes, set on the backdrop of Medieval Kings, Kingdoms, Knights, Evil Rulers and Dragons.

Made in the USA
Charleston, SC
20 May 2015